It's Okay
to be Gay

— 𝕲𝖔𝖉

It's Okay
to be Gay

— God

**How man rewrote Scripture
to justify his bigotry**

By Shirley J Foor

INTERROBANG

Bradenton, Florida

Library of Congress Cataloging in Publications Data
ISBN 979-8-9891662-0-6
Christian Books & Bibles > Bible Study
Criticism & Interpretation
Religion & Spirituality > Worship & Devotion > Faith
Christian Books > Bible Study

Published by Shirley J Foor
Interrobang, Bradenton, Florida
First edition

This is a work of nonfiction.
Opinions expressed here are those of the author.
Edited by Mark Mathes
Cover and Interior Design by Nancy Koucky, NRK Designs

In memory of Martin,
my gay high-school friend who could not rise above the abuse
of the narrow-minded folk in our small community one more time.
He committed suicide days after delivering a wedding gift to me.

In memory, too, of my gay brother, Dennis,
who found a safe place to be himself,
rather than following through on his thoughts of suicide.

**Other Books
by Shirley Foor**

Confound It!
A collection of recollections

From Smoke Signals to Sealing Wax
A collection of recollections
Volume Two

Prevenient Grace
God's gift of spiritual breadcrumbs.

Contact Shirley:

challengernow@yahoo.com

7322 Manatee Ave. W. #122
Bradenton, FL. 34209-3441

*Some people do not
want to think.
If one thinks,
one must reach conclusions,
and conclusions
are not always pleasant.*

— Helen Keller

Table of Contents

Author
Shirley J Foor

Shirley Foor began as a freelance writer when she was a young stay-at-home mom. When her husband broke his back, she became the breadwinner for her family of six. Shirley was hired as a features writer at The Daily Dispatch, in Illinois, a local newspaper. As her skills improved, she advanced to a beat reporter, to bureau chief, and to assistant editor of the regional department. She was declared unqualified and denied a promotion to regional editor but received a timely invitation to interview for the city editor's position at The Bradenton Herald in Florida. She moved her family to Florida to become the first female city editor and then the first female managing editor at The Herald. After 20 years in journalism, Shirley retired. She continues to write and to regularly publish creative-nonfiction stories for an email list of family and friends. In addition to writing, Shirley also is a photographer, beginning as a photojournalist to improve her strength as a journalist. She also has published three creative-nonfiction books of common daily experiences that touch us all. *It's Okay to be Gay* is her first major nonfiction work and is based upon her years of journalistic practices. At age 75, she graduated, magna cum laude, from Eckerd College, with a BA in Creative Writing.

Introduction

This book, *It's Okay to be Gay,* is for you.

You, the homosexual, a child of God, whose life has been threatened and sullied by the "Men of God" with their deadly falsehood that God condemns you.

You, the homosexual child of God who lives a life in the shadows because you fear being discovered and ridiculed.

You, the believer among the prejudiced God Wannabes and their followers who promote the premise that God disapproves of any of His children.

You, the judgmental child of God who repeats the malicious gossip from church friends about how God reviles homosexuals.

You, the beleaguered parents of a homosexual child, who have suffered the pain of believing that your child has sinned against God because someone you trusted has told you that nonsense.

You, the person who has a relationship with her God and asks herself, "If God is the God of love and mercy, how could He even have thought about creating something or someone to be scorned, abused, purposefully cast away from Him? If I believe, why do I listen to the cruel comments of religious friends, instead of holding firmly to God's faithful promise?"

This book is for anyone who has fallen into the trap of believing that there is something wrong with any of God's children.

My frame of reference is American Christianity and the falsehoods it has been promoting for centuries. Christianity is all I have known over my decades, but I have learned from my research that man has made the persecution of homosexuals a universal disease in every culture.

Man's unholy abuse, misuse, and hold over humankind's view of God's plan for homosexuals and same-sex couples is about to meet a much different perspective. I haven't bought into man's self-serving propaganda. I have avoided the prejudice pitfall by seeking an answer to a logical question: If God created everything and said that everything was good, then how did the homosexuals slip through His fingers? The answer is, they didn't.

Here's a quick view of why It's Okay to be Gay:

- It's okay to be gay. God said so, long before the days of the New Testament.

- Man's literal interpretations have for centuries led him astray about two of his coveted prizes: his head-ship, his God granted control, over women and God's condemnation of homosexuals. The one affects his perception of the other, and both have affected our view of many scriptures. Man has willfully altered Scripture meet his needs, not the promises of the New Covenant, and to call out homosexuals.

- The oft quoted scriptures in Leviticus do not mean what man has preached from his base of prejudice and his literal translation of ancient text. In 1983, man has distorted the Leviticus Scripture by imposing 20th century language upon the text. The revision diverts our attention away from man's abominable sexual attention to boys. Man corrupted this Scripture by inappropriately imposing current language and atti-tudes upon the texts in the Old and New testaments.

- Sodom and Gomorrah had nothing to do with homo-sexuality, even though man has so keenly distorted God's Word to make it seem so.

- The word homosexual, the word for a same-sex relationship and for the person who is not heterosexual, did not appear in the Bible until 1946.

- Homosexual was not a word that could have been used in God's ancient Scripture. It entered the English language in 1868, the 19th century.

- Individuals do not "choose" to be homosexuals, according to a comprehensive report in Science magazine.

- God anointed and celebrated same-sex relationships in the books of Ruth and 1 Samuel.

- God's homosexual children are right with God and worthy of his grace and mercy.

- There are two ways to interpret the Bible: Man's way (literal) and God's (historical, relevant to the language, culture, and mores of the time in which the texts were written). The difference is critical to understanding Scripture as it was intended.

- The research for this story is available to you. I have used books written by scholars. I have compared Scripture from many bibles. Online, I found research papers from scholars. I asked question after question to learn where the consistent and the persistent body of evidence lay. I have done what anyone who wants to know if man is teaching is the truth can do.

- I have based my research upon what God said, not man's literal interpretations of God's word. However, man's literal interpretations of God's words did help me to define my search.

Bottom line in all of this? Man's pursuit of homosexual's serves Satan and does not bring glory to God.

∽

Now, let's talk. Yes, talk. Although you are reading these words in your place of comfort, not talking with me on my porch in small-town Florida, the words have been written just for you.

Because you are reading this, you have some interest in the truth of God's plan for same-sex couples, male or female.

Or maybe you are belligerent. The words, "It's okay to be gay," anger you. Your brain repeats the long-held nonsense that God would never have allowed this to be true. You have believed this falsehood. Yes, the falsehood, that man has preached since at least 1946, when the word first appeared in 1 Corinthians, then added to 1 Timothy. In any case, I am casting a long shadow of doubt over this tedious Christian hypocrisy.

However, if your mind remains open to new information, some logic presented in *It's Okay to be Gay* may give you some new insight. You may come to challenge your belief in man's dramatic, Christian performance art about God's homosexual children. Especially the words from the Scripture parrots who perform so well from their sacred script. They know Scripture, but do not embrace and live the promise of the New Covenant, under which we Christians are bound to live since Christ died on the cross.

Because *It's Okay to be Gay* is a sensitive topic, long maligned by misinformation, we need to talk, one-to-one. Talking with you, not "at you," about the gallons of bottled bilge water we have consumed in the "name of God" for decades, and why these sinful, yes, sinful, views have been foist upon any of God's children. Always in the name of God.

Beginning with those thoughts, let's hang the meat of truth on the bones of man's malevolent misinformation. Contrary to God's decree that man and woman share joint responsibility in their new world, man has restated specific scriptures to gain prominence and power. He has declared his mythical headship over women and his belief that God made a mistake in creating homosexuals. As a result, man bears responsibility for the immoral wrongs caused by these ignorant and self-serving assertions. For instance, man's belief that he is greater than woman has prevented him from seeing the pivotal importance of the Book of Ruth in God's plan. Although women have indeed suffered under man's egotism, *It's Okay to be Gay* focuses on man's favorite whipping posts: the homosexuals whom man has wrongly singled out for his persistent abuse.

Parents of gay children also have suffered boundless and unjustified Bible-shaming by so-called Christians who profess to serve God. Still, these Christian men, whom we trust to provide the truth of Scripture, are relentless in peddling their pernicious poppycock.

You might ask, "What about the women?" I agree. The spreading of prejudice is not limited to men. Ages ago, man declared himself the righteous authority in our world and has used his misinterpretation of Scripture to wrongly relegate women to silence in the shadows. To speak only when spoken to. Stifling thought and opinions because man wrongly insists that the "Bible says" woman must remain silent. And, so, as a rule, women repeat, without thought, whatever their particular God Wannabe has said because, well, man knows best. According to man, woman must not speak independent thought. Over time, man has persuaded us that on things biblical only his words count.

Who am I to be questioning man's words, man's motives, you ask? I am a servant of God, acting on His behalf. I am the mother of five children, a retired journalist with 20 years' experience, and, currently, a writer and editor. Three years ago, He stirred the Holy Spirit to direct my thinking and my writing. He has talked to me in the dead of night, with new words, new viewpoints, new information to be included in this story.

For instance, the word "headship" came to me very early one morning. Then, "man's headship". Because I possessed only the common knowledge of the Bible, I thought, "Oh, yeah. Man thinks he is the boss of me." And every other woman. Wrong thinking. When you read Chapter One, you will begin to understand that man is not in charge of woman at all. Man has extrapolated his phony authority by spreading false information often enough, authoritatively enough, that we believe his words. We believe because we foolishly and implicitly trust man to do the right thing on our behalf.

I am a woman. And, as you know, man has always owned the bully pulpit and determined what we know about the Bible, God, and His plan for all of creation. Bully is the operative word. Words from a forthright woman such as I only annoy the bully. As my words herein are bound to do.

Yes, I wanted the cup to pass from me. I knew in every nerve that man would not take kindly to my questioning him, even on God's behalf. I have no interest in the whining that will rise from the men who have made hay on their dishonesty. A God Wannabe questions everyone who speaks a viewpoint different from his, anything that does not come from his mouth. However, one must not shrink from God's will. A bunch of Christian platitudes for staying God's course came to mind as I resisted His call. You've heard them. "If He brings you to it, He will bring you through it," and "He never gives you more than you can handle." Yada, yada. Platitudes are cotton candy compared with the solid Scripture from Isaiah, which says, "Fear not, for I am with you." So, I forged ahead.

A few years ago, God motivated my research after He drew me to a fanciful Bible study[1] of the Book of Ruth. A friend had invited me to participate in the study at her church. I told my friend that I would think about it. I love my friend, but I am not a fan of her denomination. I thought of ways to politely decline her invitation. God was having none of that thinking. Under duress, I joined her.

That study of Ruth fostered images of two fragile women, Ruth and Naomi, uncertain of their futures, and a mythical love affair between Ruth and Boaz, and their wedding, which Scripture never mentions. In fact, the Scripture in the Book of Ruth supported very few of the author's flights of fantasy, such as a seductive, sexual assignation between Ruth and Boaz.

The experience troubled me for several reasons. First were the many flagrant contradictions between the premise of the study and the Scripture in Ruth. For example, the study portrayed Naomi as being angry with her daughters because they insisted that they be allowed to accompany her to Bethlehem. She wanted to dismiss them because they were being tiresome. Scripture does not support that idea. Not a single word suggests strife among the women. Second were the subjective and derisive comments from women who were raised in "good Christian homes." They prattled on about how Ruth was judged for being a Moabitess. Scripture showed the opposite: Boaz and the community respected Ruth for being a good daughter-in-law to Naomi. Moab is not mentioned.

As I pursued my research, God gave me a larger purpose: research man's self-determined contention that the God of all things erred when He included homosexuals in His design. Homosexuals, according to man's assertion, are an abomination to the Lord and should be denied all rights to God's love, mercy, and grace. From my research, Ruth is the story of God's public anointing of a same-sex relationship. Ruth also is one of only two books of female prominence in the Old Testament, which implies greater depth of purpose for Ruth.

My research has been stunning in its revelations and disgusting because it lays bare man's manipulation of ancient words to satisfy his relentless need to be superior. Same-sex, homosexual, relationships are not new to history. Nor did they just pop into prominence when man coined the word. History records the presence of homosexuals since the beginning of humankind. You can easily research this fact. With all of this, the meat of hypocrisy and the deceit perpetrated by man lie ready to hang on the bones of truth.

I cannot know for sure, but I shall hazard a guess that God has grown weary of man misusing His words to persecute His children. So, He called me to this task of providing a new perspective, one in opposition to the plentiful myths of man. The words and the attitudes herein are largely His. I have been His scribe. Whenever I slipped into my bare-bones journalistic approach to my writing, He admonished me to "tell the story you have learned."

If you have worked for God, not just "done God's work," you know that He is unrelenting. He does not settle for what we consider "good enough."

I freely admit that He really ticked me off a couple of times, mostly because I thought He was asking me to lay bare too many of man's self-serving biases. Among them is man's penchant for bending the meaning of Scripture to serve himself, for one. For another is man's being in league with Satan to divert our scorn from him to the hapless homosexuals who have fallen prey to man's arrogance. For yet another is man's obsession with his manhood (penis).

It is fruitless to argue with God. He always wins.

My research shows that man has perpetuated a self-righteous agenda. In executing his agenda, he has dismissed women from his presence, except for his occasional animal need of a woman's services. Even though God made man and woman partners to build His world, man has come up with a bunch of cockeyed reasons for why he is the superior creation: God made and named him first; woman was taken from his side (will get to that gem later); God made woman to "help" him, which is the sorriest of excuses for usurping God's authority.

To maintain his questionable dominion over woman, man misinterpreted the Greek word God used to describe woman's role with Adam. The Greek word, from the original text, the inclusion of which in this text is irrelevant to our understanding, means "a strength corresponding to him (Adam)." Woman was to be man's full partner in the new world.

However, in order to assert his unauthorized dominance, man has translated the Greek word to mean "helper," which implies a subordinate or servant. This misrepresentation of God's intent changed the trajectory of His plan. Man has mistranslated out of existence God's stated equality between the female Adam and the male Adam.

Ah, you think I am being too hard on man, too judgmental. Please! Any human being with the sense that God gave a goose, as my beloved grandmother used to say, would recognize that man has blatantly, persistently called God a liar. Genesis declares that God made all things; man says God screwed up.

Considering the evil, man has visited upon God's homosexual children, I think the words herein are nothing, if not generous and thoughtful. Considering the perverted, hateful initiatives currently being promulgated by the political versions of the God Wannabes, my words are meek. So, while you assess your thoughts, assess, too, man's role in the steady distortion of God's word.

For clarity and consistency, I use the word "man" throughout my story. I use the word as a collective noun from the historical perspective, not a pejorative one.

After all, man has shaped everything we know, or think we know, or believe we know about God, about the Bible, and about God's intentions. Man wrote the many books of the Bible, presumably with the inspired word from God. However, we have only man's unfaithful word for that assertion. In one case, which will be made clear later, we know the text is not divinely inspired.

Man has tweaked many versions of the Bible to suit the schisms in religious denominations and the opinions of the inter-preters/translators. More than 60 English versions of the Bible are available to us. Add to that number the many, many versions in the languages of other nations, and the opportunities for man's misinterpretation are endless.

Additionally, man has misinterpreted the statement of the Apostle Paul that woman must remain quiet, to mean that only man may preach the words Paul has written. We have only the male perspective of Scripture. However, several female evangelists have sought answers to the discrepancies they have encountered and now preach the message of the New Testament.

On the other hand, man spews word soup, a slumgullion of misinformation, lazy, literal interpretations, and unclear thought, sustained by an elite group of false prophets.

They insist that God, the God of love who made everything in this world, would condemn any of His creations. Seriously? How preposterous!

Do you truly believe it is reasonable for any true Christian to consider, much less promote, the idea that God did willfully create a group of His children to be objects of humankind's scorn? Get a grip, please. Remember? You say you believe that God does not make mistakes or create junk. Does this viewpoint apply only to "junk" of which you approve?

Another term needs some perspective: Christian. We believe we know who the Christians are, but do we really?

I put Christians into two categories. In the one, we have the Christian who walks among his brothers and sisters in Christ, meets them where they are, and attends to the least among them. He is humble and heeds Jesus' lesson when ". . . the King shall answer and say unto them, Verily I say unto you, inasmuch as ye have done it unto one of the least of these my brethren, ye have done it unto me." King James Version (KJV)

On the other hand, we have the God Wannabes who ignore this admonition. Generally, we consider this Scripture in terms of doing good works among God's most vulnerable children. However, those words are a two-edged sword: When you treat my children poorly, you treat Me equally as poorly. When you abuse any of My children, you abuse Me. That edge appears to elude the God Wannabes.

The God Wannabes are all about themselves. They call the people to them in elaborate buildings or on television. They live in mansions on massive acreage. As God's representatives, many of whom receive money in abundance, without evidence that they have invested any portion of their abundance in God's mission.

Their Christian service to the poor, the downtrodden, or any of God's less-fortunate children is negligible. They judge. They warn. Their actions show that they have forgotten God's commandments: Love the Lord your God with all your heart and with all your soul and with all your mind. This is the first and greatest commandment. And the second is like it: Love your neighbor as yourself. (Matthew 22:37-39) The laws of the Old Testament, not the promises of the New Covenant, remain man's authority.

Yes, God did refer to a gathering of followers of His word. He had small gatherings in mind. Not buildings where thousands gather to pay homage to the man in the pulpit or the television stage. And to contribute to that "church" in faith, without any idea of where your faith offering goes. Man has transformed the intimate and the personal association with God into the grand and the profitable, even profane, houses of worship and profit centers.

I must repeat here that I am not talking about all large gatherings and prophets. However, Google your favorite man of God to see how and where the money you so freely give is used. How does he serve God? The websites celebritynetworth.com and Wikipedia.com provide starting points for additional information on your favorite evangelist. You will discover how closely these men hold their wealth for themselves.

For example, one very prominent man of God contributes to pigmies in some distant land. Not that pigmies don't need help, but meeting their needs doesn't take much from his ample coffers. Furthermore, history shows that pigmies prefer living away from humans in their jungle homes. Another God Wannabe charges a fixed fee for his preaching in his huge gathering hall and publishes many books for which his followers pay again. It remains unclear where, or if, the money from his ventures is used for God's greater good. His website does not list any mission work in which he engages. He just writes books and collects the money. I could name these God Wannabes, but it is my experience that when we discover deception on our own terms, the message sticks with us.

My son admonishes me for my thinking. He says that if these men bring even one person closer to God from their massive gatherings, then they have done their job. I say, a Christian who has a relationship with God can accomplish the same walking down a street in town or sitting in a restaurant. This Christian also does not expect a reward for meeting someone's need where it is.

The Women of God, new to inviting us to draw nearer to God, preach from the New Testament and invest their donations toward enriching the lives of others. To be sure, I do not attribute goodness to all female evangelists nor avarice to all men. All is God's province. Women do, however, bring a more God-like approach to their ministries, promoting health-care programs, providing wells and clean water, and building schools for the education of the children, especially of the girls.

If you believe I am being too critical of those who call themselves men of God, spend some time, even a minimum of online research, to learn about your favorite man. You will be surprised, if not appalled, to know where your faithful donations have been going, or not going.

Finally, *It's Okay to be Gay* is not intended to be a treatise. Libraries are full of important, skillfully written books on the topic of the church and homosexuality. *It's Okay to be Gay* is a more distinctive story, commissioned, if you will, by God. I have written much of the original text in longhand, on reams of paper because writing in longhand is personal, and the practice keeps my thoughts grounded. I have written on my porch in Gulf Coast Florida, where my thoughts are always in tune with God's osprey and hawks, His rain, and His wind. Even the brazen and annoying squirrel that runs across the screened enclosure keeps me in His will.

I call this a story, a nonfiction story. Stories are personal, like the "just-right porridge" that suited Goldilocks. Word porridge provides easy-to-digest facts and the comfortable background that goes with the facts. You can think as you digest. Sermons may well have the ingredients of satisfying porridge, but they are not necessarily personal. The messages generally are "sold" and served cold. A sermon also is easy to dismiss.

And the haranguing from your well-meaning Christian friend who insists that you need to do something about your sinful, abominable homosexual child? Well, that noise is so far from being personal that she could be speaking in a foreign tongue. Although face-to-face, the encounter is too hot, too contentious to be anything but stinging gruel, straight from the stove.

This story is intended to be more like one friend talking to another. We humans learn best in quiet conversation when we can weigh, consider, and question what we are learning. The story is based upon facts. Facts from the historical perspective of the Bible. Facts easily learned from general-knowledge sources. Facts researched by scholars, the women and the men called to help unravel the web of deception, misinformation, and misperceptions in man's thinking and preaching. They also help those of us who are seeking clarity in the words we hear.

God did not get the "same sex" thing wrong. Nothing in the Bible, until 1946, when man did some of his infamous "tweaking," supports man's denunciation of homosexuals. The word homosexual was coined many millennia after any scripture was written.

By now, the God Wannabe reading this is searching for Scripture, any Scripture, to disprove or to discount what I have written. After all, man has been our Bible authority for eons, and he will not give up his long-held place in his hierarchy or the patriarchy without a vigorous scrap. Our researched assertions are bound to inflame his defense tactics. Facts can be ugly or beautiful, irksome or revealing, depending upon one's intellectual and personal bent. Still, fact remains fact, a constant that I depended upon during my 20 years as a journalist.

Epictetus, a Greek philosopher who believed that individuals should examine and control their thoughts and actions, said, "It is impossible for a man to learn what he thinks he already knows."

Is it impossible for you to learn?

Let's test your spirit for embracing new information.

On his visit to Africa in January of 2023, the press asked Pope Francis about his views on the world criminalizing LGBTI people. According to Gerald West, a professor of biblical studies at the University of KwaZulu-Natal, Pope Francis replied, "This is not right. Persons with homosexual tendencies are children of God. God loves them. God accompanies them . . . condemning a person like this is a sin. Criminalizing people with homosexual tendencies is an injustice."[2]

(Note: LGBTI is Lesbian, Gay, Bisexual, Transgender, and Intersex. Intersexuality is an umbrella term used to describe a wide range of natural bodily variations. And those variations are not fabricated.)

The Pope later tidied his comments because the opinionated among the cassock crew had worked themselves into a lather. He masterfully soothed their pious attitudes with words that fitted their attention to Catholic church dogma. He did not, however, alter the tenor of his message to the assembled before him in Africa. He said what he said.

"Some of these Catholics may argue that Pope Francis's approach to LGBTI matters is a misinterpretation of Scripture (or the Bible). ". . . The Bible always is interpreted by our churches through their particular theological lenses.

"As a biblical scholar, I would suggest that church leaders who use their cultures and theology to exclude homosexuals don't read Scripture carefully. Instead, they allow their patriarchal fears to distort it, seeking to find in the Bible proof-texts that will support attitudes of exclusion."

Professor West has capsulized the thesis of this story. In the following chapters, we will talk about man's many "proof texts" that have perverted our thinking about his place in God's plan, the homosexuals, and God's public anointing of same-sex relationships and homosexuality. We will talk about the pivotal role God granted to Ruth and Naomi and to David and Jonathan.

Author's Note: A couple of points may cause you some unrest in your reading. First might be the fact that my text addresses the male homosexuals to the exclusion of the females. Man's contrived outrage over homosexuals centers on the males. Yes, there are female homosexuals, but they do not threaten the male hierarchy or patriarchy and, therefore, are not much for man to worry about. So, I have centered my thoughts and comments on the males.

The other topic is the use of Lord and LORD. These words appear in spiritual quotations from the Bible or in text from the scholars. The difference is specific. The first is a reference to the Lord, as in asking for a favor or giving thanks, for example. The second, LORD, is used in the Old Testament and means God's name, there and then. It is specific to the time and place.

Examining the Trash Talk

What travesties have been wrought in the name of God.

I sit here between the silence of sadness and the turmoil of anger, wondering how I could have allowed man to bamboozle me, as he has bamboozled and hornswoggled us all since God created him. This whole flap about homosexuals is less about how God made a mistake, as man contends, than it is about man's intense need to protect his place in the hierarchy of maleness. The symbol of his maleness, as you will learn, exceeds his allegiance to God.

God is simple, a contradiction to man's contrived interpretations. Love me. Love your neighbor as yourself. Do unto others as you would have them do unto you. The Holy Spirit lives in you. Jesus Christ lives in you. Do not fear for I am with you always.

I ask, what more do you need to know? Man has created tortured interpretations of God's words for his aggrandizement, which is an indication that God is not central in man's mind or in his actions.

As I researched Leviticus and Sodom and Gomorrah and all of the other Scriptures man chooses and uses to prove his questionable superiority and his judgment of homosexuals, it seemed clear that man has been duplicitous. He has directed our attention away from his foul service to the devil. Yes, you read correctly. Man's service to Satan.

If man is not glorifying God, then, whom is he serving? If man speaks against God's creation, as he does when he vilifies an entire group of God's children, whom is he serving? If man riles his followers to condemn those same people, is he glorifying God? Isn't our purpose as God's children to glorify Him in everything we do? That, too, is a simple concept.

Nevertheless, scholars have spent decades attempting to prove the negative: how man's claim that Scripture supports his contention that homosexuals are an abomination to the Lord cannot be true. Yet, the Book of Ruth is the antithesis to man's premise. Why not start there? In Ruth, God publicly declares that He is anointing same-sex relationships. Perhaps the more pertinent question to answer is, "How do the Book of Ruth and the story of David in 1 and 2 Samuel demonstrate the premise that God anointed same-sex relationships?"

Many questions rise from the contradictions in man's arguments. Not the least among those questions is: How can a man of God so brazenly manipulate God's word to elevate himself and to condemn others? Not just in one way, but through two inextricably linked bits of history.

First is man's manipulation and literal interpretation of Scripture to persuade us that God gave him a "headship," the right to dominate women, and a vaunted sense of authority.

Second is his belief that his self-proclaimed headship gives him the right not only to subjugate women but also to disparage homosexuals. He declares that homosexuals are the fallen children of God, and that the mistake is God's. The evidence of God's plan speaks for itself in Ruth and in 1 and 2 Samuel. If man had taken to heart those declarations, we would not be talking about this now.

Furthermore, man's relentless contention, diligently promoted over the centuries, is like a millennia-old game of "telephone." Man's false premise has persisted because man has listened to man and listened to man and repeated and massaged man's message. Each repetition is restated according to the listener's understanding of what he has heard, then he repeats his own interpretation of what was said. Without man gaining some understanding of the purpose of the Scripture when it was written, we have only his faulty literal viewpoint, which inappropriately overlays current customs, culture, and language onto ancient Biblical text.

And through this passing along of man's flawed interpretations, no one asks, "If God is the God of love, how can we direct our hate and prejudice toward his children?"

Before we continue this part of the story, I need to define what "man of God" we are talking about. As I mentioned in the Introduction, there are at two prominent types of Christians who are as far removed from each other as the east is from the west. Our emphasis from now on is the God-Wannabe crowd that exalts the leader who expects adoration and discipleship from his loyal followers. His followers believe, without question, every word from their oracle.

The God Wannabe insists that his selective interpretations of God's words are indeed the word of God. The God Wannabes have created a batch of special mule muffins, carefully shaped from the foul ingredients of prejudice, hate, hubris, and ignorance chosen over true knowledge. For centuries, man has refined the recipe of his arrogant interpretations, misuse of Scripture, and misdirection. Because we have trusted man, we have consumed his vile concoction as truth and washed it down with bottles of man's tasteless-and-vile bilge water we have named "trust." We have been duped in the name of honor and trust to satisfy man's need to be more important than the God who created him.

Since the moment that God created him, man has been a proper dunce about his role in the greater scheme of things. He has been unable to set himself firmly in the service of the Lord. In too many instances to count, man has forgotten whose words rule. Then, to show himself as someone whom he is not, he self-righteously founds "The Church of Enlightened Thought," for example, and names himself pastor of that church. He preaches from his own gospel, determined by his literal translations of Scripture, which his followers trust and believe. This conceit is especially true regarding man's woeful misunderstanding of his role as God declared in Genesis.

After we dispense with a couple of trays of mule muffins and several tureens of slumgullion, we'll get to the purpose of my narrative, to show the Book of Ruth's pivotal role in God's plan and His anointing of same-sex relationships. The story of David and Jonathan in 1 and 2 Samuel, also ignored by man, strengthens the assertion of Ruth's purpose.

The first tray carries man's gruel of his insatiable need for attention and his malicious betrayal of trust, the basic idea of trust that is expected with his message. We expect, because we trust, that man will have done his homework and created his sermon from God's words, not from his imagination or his opinion.

Man's self-importance and his singular ownership of God's word has shaped every facet of what we know as religion and our understanding of God. I say here that the religions of today should not be confused with God's call to each of us to follow Him. Man has created many religions—prominent denominations and independent alliances. No one interpretation of the Bible satisfies man, and no one church keeps him front and center on the Christian stage, so he creates his own church that features his interpretation of Scripture.

Religions and denominations are man's construct and are fraught with rules, manmade rules that have rules. The rules define who may or may not wholly participate in the liturgy of that denomination. God, on the other hand, embraces all who seek Him.

The Hartford Seminary[3] reports that 217 denominations and some 35,000 independent or nondenominational groups exist in the United States. Moreover, some of the bibles contain different books among religions. For instance, the Catholic Bible contains 77 books in the Old Testament; the Protestant Bible contains 66. Both bibles have 27 books each in the New Testament, and they are the same 27 books.

The huge gatherings to which the God Wannabe delivers his

message, also are of man's construct. In fact, the God Wannabe makes his living by rousing these gatherings to the climax of opening purse or wallet.

Neither God nor Jesus asked for man to create huge worship centers nor massive congregations with rules for who is in and who is prohibited from being a full member of said congregation. God saw His "church" as a universal concept in which God's view is simple: "Where two or three are gathered in my name, there I am also." (Matthew 18:20) Man has other ideas.

John Pavlovitz, a writer and pastor in North Carolina, says that, at the Last Supper Jesus commands His disciples to remember him whenever they break bread together. "He is not telling them to establish a weekly worship service or to create a rigid liturgy or to institute a sacrament. He is commanding them not to forget Him; to live together and to eat and to remember. No sanctuary is necessary for this. This is a fully portable experience."[4] And yet, man's many churches seem to contradict that idea. They represent everything that Jesus did not seek, including intercessors, such as the priests in Catholic churches that separate us from our direct and personal fellowship with God. The intercessions benefit them greatly.

If my tone of voice sounds cranky, that's because I am cranky. In some places my words are irreverent, even snarky or derisive. Some of man's behaviors are as quaintly humorous as they are offensive. My charity and spirit of generosity for man ended as my research for this story grew. Man's abuse of his trust, both God's trust in him to do the right thing and his breach of trust with us, offends.

But I am getting ahead of myself. There is much more to man's aggrandizement and his association to the Book of Ruth and of 1 Samuel, which has basically paralyzed our understanding of God and His unambiguous plan. All is all, and everything is everything. These concepts are uniquely and wholly God's.

The second tray carries the huge mule muffin of man's

presumed headship over women.

During 25 years of marriage and 20 years as a journalist, when journalism was absolutely a man's world, I heard the unending crass and brainless comments from men that were meant to remind me of my appropriate place in man's world. I shall not repeat them to satisfy the men who have said them or thought them, or to prick the memories of the women who have suffered under them in embarrassment, shame, and stinging insult.

The men in my daily life had assumed an inappropriate authority over women, as a product of man's consistent publication and blatant misuse of God's word. As a woman, I was invisible and voiceless. In much of our world today, women continue to be invisible and voiceless.

When the Supreme Court of the United States (SCOTUS) overturned Roe Vs. Wade, a 50-year-old constitutional protection for a woman's right to have an abortion, those men told women to sit down and shut up. We have no voice in our lives. The justices have spoken. They would decide our health-care rights. As a group, men have joined into decisions among state legislatures to deny women the right to her own health-care choices. These decisions reduce women from man's equal to mere chattel and render women legally voiceless.

Nevertheless, God's insistence and His words in the Book of Ruth have given me a voice. And I laugh. For centuries, man has unabashedly distributed his propaganda. Now, as a woman, as a mother, and as a retired journalist, I have been charged with providing a new perspective of man's propaganda. My text to start this discussion is, *"Male-Female Equality and Male Headship (Genesis 1-3)."* The piece is from a series: *"Recovering Biblical Manhood and Womanhood,"* written by Raymond C. Ortlund Jr.[5]

For the record, I did not choose this document to single out the writer. No, I chose it because the writer had gathered the many bits and pieces of man's wet dreams into one place. I was hard pressed to ignore this bonanza of discovery.

However, my first thought was to direct the author to return with one page of clear God said citations to support his argument.

Ortlund's cheap stew of words required a strong strainer to separate any real worth from his wishful thinking. The author started well enough. He acknowledged that God's words in Genesis 1:27 were fact. "So, God created man in his own image, in the image of God he created him; male and female he created them." He further acknowledged that in verse 28. "God blessed them and said to them . . ." "Them" being the operative word. Then Ortlund slides off the rails of good sense. He asserts that God then named humans man, therefore, that "foreshadows the male headship."

Oh, my. We need to explore Ortlund's moment of fantasy. Five words—Us, Our, them, everything, and all—will become prominent.

Ortlund cites the New International Version (NIV) for the Scripture (Genesis 1:26-27) in which, he states, that God did indeed name us humans as man. Normally speaking, the word man used in this way embraces all of us.

Then, Ortlund begins his strange logic, a logic embraced by many a God Wannabe, to project and to protect his presumed male-headship position. "God did not name the human race 'woman.' If woman had been the more appropriate and illuminating designation, no doubt God would have used it . . . He called us 'man' which anticipates the male headship brought out clearly in chapter two (of Genesis) . . ."

Ortlund can assert whatever he wants, but, in my view, only man "anticipates the male headship," no matter where he believes it appears in any Bible. God would not and did not give up His authority over His children.

Now, I ask, just why and when did God allow, appoint, or invite anyone to be an intermediary between Him and His children? Yes, the Catholic Church has profited well from its practice of selling intercessions, priest generated prayers, on behalf of its parishioners. However, nowhere has God conferred confer a headship upon any man, not even the Catholics.

The New King James Version (NKJV), Genesis 5:2, reinforces the words in Genesis 1; "He created them male and female, and blessed them and called them Mankind in the day they were created." Mankind. No male headship is implied in the word mankind. The NIV also uses this terminology. The KJV, however, added a finer point on the equality of man and woman. The Scripture says, "Male and female created he them; and blessed them, and called their name Adam, in the day when they were created," which makes them the male Adam and the female Adam.

Strangely, Ortlund included words from *Beyond the Curse: Women Called to Ministry,* by Aida Bensanon Spencer.[6] Rather than supporting his premise, this Scripture-based statement disproves his self-serving premise. From my perspective, Spencer's words blow the crown of headship off Ortlund's bumptious head.

Spencer writes that "Male and female are together needed to reflect God's image . . .There is no possibility, according to [Genesis 1:26-27], that Adam, the male, could by himself reflect the nature of God. Neither is it possible for Adam, the female, by herself to reflect God's nature. Male and female are needed to reflect God's nature."

To give Spencer's viewpoint a fair review I add this: Ortlund formed his thesis about man's headship from Genesis 5:2 in which man reports what God had created, not what God said He had created in 1:26.

Then, Ortlund becomes confused and, once again, uses Spencer's reference to Genesis 1: 26-27 to support his argument. Then God said, "Let Us make man in Our image, according to Our likeness; let them have dominion over the fish of the sea, over the birds of the air, and over the cattle, over all the earth and over every creeping thing that creeps on the earth." Us and Our are key words. "Let Us create man in 'Our likeness'" implies that God is both man and woman, equally, which supports Spencer's assertion.

Full disclosure: other bibles use the designations of mankind, humans, and human beings for the universal man. No headship implied there, either. Basically, man has pompously, cavalierly interpreted away the equality between woman and man that God had ordained.

Brett Kunkle,[7] writing in the *"Challenge Response: The Bible Says Men Are Superior to Women,"* harkens to Ephesians 5:22, one of man's go-to Scriptures to support his headship theory. Kunkle says that man has, at the very least, misunderstood the Bible's teachings. To explain, he references Ephesians 5:21, which says, to both Adams, ". . . and be subject to one another in the fear of Christ." He follows that with Ephesians 5:22, which says, "Wives, be subject to your own husbands as to the Lord, for the husband is head of the wife as Christ is the head of the Church." This sends the headship hunters into untold rapture.

However, Kunkle further explains that Christ, as head of the church, sacrificed much for the church. Man, acting as Christ, therefore, must sacrifice much on behalf of his wife. As with others of man's version of Scripture, Ortlund conveniently omits the "sacrifice much" on behalf of his wife part when he refers to Ephesians 5:22.

Kunkle clarifies the intent of the Scripture that man has interpreted to claim his superiority over women. "When we think headship, we think leadership, we think worldly view, right? Well, 'I have authority over you. I tell you what to do. You listen to me. I give you orders.' That's not the biblical view. That's not the model of Christ. Christianity dignifies women all throughout Scripture and gives them a whole different status. It's actually Christianity that brings the value of women to the forefront. So, does the Bible teach that men are superior to women? Absolutely not." [8]

Philip B. Payne,[9] in *"The Bible Teaches the Equal Standing of Man and Woman,"* sorts out the business of woman being a "helper" to man, which is the erroneous interpretation of the Greek word that means "a strength corresponding to him (Adam)." Payne says, "Unfortunately, the (Greek) word is often translated 'helper,' which, in English, implies a subordinate or servant. Never in the Bible, however, does the (Greek) word suggest 'helper,' as in 'servant.'" Payne emphasizes that nothing in the context of any of these biblical passages warrants concluding that the word makes woman subordinate to man.

Returning to Ortlund's paper, he offers many useless paragraphs of confused thinking, but he finally brought us to a strange-but-interesting ingredient in creation, dust. This Scripture heartened Ortlund's thinking that man is superior to woman.

Genesis 2:7, NIV, says "Then the Lord God formed man from the dust of the ground and breathed into his nostrils the breath of life, and the man became a living being."

Ortlund continues with Genesis 2:21-22: "So the Lord God caused the man to fall into a deep sleep; and while he was sleeping, He took one of the man's ribs and then closed up the place with flesh. Then the Lord God made a woman from the rib he had taken out of the man, and he brought her to the man, and the man named her 'woman.'" This Scripture gave Ortlund great hope in his hunt for the holy grail of headship.

According to man, this sequence of actions in Scripture makes woman secondary to man. Neither Scripture nor scholars supports that theory in any manner, but man has manufactured a connection in his mind, a connection that faithful followers trust unerringly.

I offer a different point of view. So, Scripture says that Adam was created from the dust of the ground, as were all of the animals that paraded before Adam to be named.

Well, using Ortlund's logic and that of other men of like reasoning, I offer a different image of the creation of humans. Man was made of the same dust as the animals that he names, which places Adam on the same level as the other animals. Being the human animal, though, Adam does have an edge in the animal kingdom. Then, God created woman from the human, not the dust of the ground. God created woman from the real deal, as it were. To my thinking, this elevates the female Adam above the human dust bunny, the male Adam.

Before we leave the conversation of bottled bilge water, mule muffins, and slumgullion, let's add one more Scripture that sends Ortlund, and other God Wannabes into quivers and shivers of delight in their headship hunting. Genesis 2:24: "Therefore a man shall leave his father and mother and be joined to his wife, and they shall become one flesh." This proves, say the headship hunters, that God expected man to have headship. Give us a break. Please.

Looking at this from a woman's point of view, God knew, as mothers and behavioral scientists know from experience, that the boy child is slower to mature and sometimes needs a good shove to leave his momma's home cooking. God already had instructed both Adams to "go forth and multiply," and just as importantly, to become one flesh in their union. Apparently, the male Adam did not understand the memo. Now, God reinforces His words by telling the immature Adam to grow up and get out of his parent's home, find a wife, and go forth and multiply. Do the job for which God anointed you. No headship is implied, except in man's mind. The phrase "become one flesh" should have ended man's delusion.

One other thing worth noting in that Scripture is that father and mother are equal in the statement. God does not say, "Leave the head of your father's house and the woman who reports to him." In God's eyes, and in Scripture, father and mother are one. Just as God expects man to join to his wife as one flesh and be one in creating a family. No headship is stated or implied in Genesis 2:24.

Man insists that he has been granted a headship, a place of prominence and authority. He believes this position allows him to assume authority and superiority, an authority God holds unto Himself. Only his literal misinterpretations of Scripture allow him to think that. "Let Us make man in Our image, according to Our likeness" in Genesis 1:26-27 should have nipped that fantasy in the bud, too, but man is persistent in his folly.

Man mistakenly believes that, as a God Wannabe, he has dominion over the lives of us humans, especially women and those who "choose" to become homosexuals. This brings us to the second travesty: Another concoction of mule muffins, shaped by prejudice and misuse of Scripture to condemn and to shame homosexuals.

The thing of it is, God's plan is God's plan, not man's plan or man's interpretation of God's plan.

Then, I wondered if Ortlund or any of the God Wannabes, ever think about the 10 Commandments. Especially the Third Commandment "You shall not take the name of the LORD your God in vain; for the LORD will not hold him guiltless that taketh his name in vain." Exodus 20:7.

When I was a child and thought as a child, I believed that the Third Commandment was about swearing and using God's name in a bad way. Now that I have researched the topic, I have learned that the admonition is more inclusive.

In the purpose and meaning of the Third Commandment[10], the updated version of the New Revised Standard Version (NRSV), translates the Third Commandment this way: "You shall not make wrongful use of the name of the LORD your God, for the LORD will not acquit anyone who misuses his name." The meaning of the Hebrew word was translated as "wrongfully use" and "misuse." "In vain" in other translations is "deceit; deception; malice; falsity; vanity; emptiness."

Do the Commandments not pertain to the God Wannabes?

You may think that I have spent too much time on man's hubris and his penchant for playing so freely with Scripture. Still, unless and until we understand how man influences and controls our basic understanding of God and Scripture, we cannot understand how man could have dismissed/ignored the critical, seminal nature of the Book of Ruth, and the seminal words in Samuel.

Mr. Ortlund has overlooked Jesus' words in Galatians 3:28: "There is neither Jew nor Greek, there is neither bond nor free, there is neither male nor female: for ye are all one in Christ Jesus (emphasis mine)." These words are part of the New Covenant, which vex man's plan.

It appears that God dumped a pail of cold slumgullion over man's contentions that he has a headship, and that God has no room for homosexuals. All still means all, and everything still means everything. And both definitions belong to God.

Basically, for centuries we have accepted and repeated, without question, what man has told us. How, then, can we go forward to learn the importance of the Book of Ruth without a better understanding of how man's viewpoint and motives have brought us to this point? Perhaps the better question is why, when faced with a ton of abominations about which to rail, has man manufactured a pointless conflict? We shall examine that answer in Chapter 3.

First, let's look at some of man's ignorant myths that have shaped our long-held beliefs, prejudices, and man's fantasies.

Exploring the Ignorant Myths

Facts do not cease to exist because they are ignored
—Aldous Huxley.

No statement could be truer when it comes to the anti-homosexual religious folk. They don't like those "perverts," and, by George, they're gonna make the Bible Scripture support their assumptions. (This is the author's observation, based upon decades of watching and listening to these determined God Wannabes. ("They are disgusting!" "They should not be allowed in our church!" "Homosexuals are unnatural!")

Regardless of how carefully the zealots pick apart select Scripture to prove their misguided points, the fact remains: The Bible does not support their prejudice. The word homosexual, first coined by the Germans[11] in 1868. The word was in use in 1909 but not included in the Merriam Webster dictionary until 1923, as a medical term, meaning "A morbid sexual passion for one of the same sex."[12] It does not appear in any Bible until 1946. No matter how hard man wants us to believe otherwise, the facts of original Scripture speak on their own merits.

Where do my words fit into this story? I am an ordinary Christian who undertook this task in consternation. I could not understand how man could ignore the truth of the Book of Ruth and the truth of Scripture in Genesis, and the truth in Samuel. Or, worse yet, that man would dare to question God's plan.

As I have said, these are the same folk who so pompously

and glibly declare that God does not make mistakes or make junk. Then, they undertake a dogged campaign of muckraking designed to disenfranchise His children by declaring that homosexuals are a gross mistake. How can a true Christian question God's work? By what level of hubris does man call God incompetent, even wrong, in His creation of homosexuals?

To make sense of the mean-spirited contentions of the so-called "conservative Christians," I have read the work of many scholars. I also have watched many, way too many, "men of God" on television. Some seemed sincere in their messages. Some were zealots who, being so sure of God's word in their ignorance, hollered about their faith and their assurance of God's plan for their audience. The louder the message, the more I wondered about the message. A couple of them were simply sleazy, sexist old men, who were, from my perspective, "on the hustle," for those donations. Their words insulted the women in their audience and pleased the men, who found their sexist quips funny and applause worthy. From my perspective, this "preaching" does not resemble God's love and mercy, but the men fell for it.

In full disclosure, I also have found the occasional source who presented the popular viewpoint, the almost combative point of view, that being homosexual is a sin. I dismissed their words from the discussion of facts. In my opinion as a journalist, their credentials as authorities on any position, other than on their prejudice, are meaningless. They carry the same weight as the credentials of the men who have founded a "church," called themselves "pastor," and preach from their literal interpretations of Scripture. They willingly and unerringly parrot the men who promulgated and preached the ignorant messages that appear in print.

What I say throughout my story is based upon the researched information provided by academically qualified Bible scholars. These are the men and the women with relevant degrees and professional intent who devote their talents to scholarship. Women and men who have studied the customs, the history, and the linguistics of the original text. The many scholars who have invested their experience and their study to bring some reality to man's contention that God created a condition of humanity that would be a sin. Not just that the person would commit sin, as we all do, but that the homosexual person exists as sin, just by being alive. What does God think about this viewpoint? I wonder.

Although the scholars are consistent in their views of the misinterpretation and the misuse of select Scriptures, Jack Rogers, in *Jesus, the Bible and Homosexuality*, clearly connected the conclusions of these scholars in three succinct sentences. "Most Christians have been told at one time or another that the Bible condemns all homosexual relationships. That view is simply incorrect. For hundreds of years the Bible has been used inappropriately to oppress people who are homosexual."[13]

Let's examine the scriptures that man believes support the popular notion that the Bible, and therefore God, condemns homosexuality. I call their interpretations the Unholy Myths.

According to my research, man consistently, persistently focuses on these specific scriptures to support his fallacious positions: Genesis 19:1-29; Judges19: 1-30; Leviticus 18:1-30; Leviticus 20:1-27; 1 Corinthians 6:9; 1 Timothy 1:10.

The scholars have arrived at a common viewpoint when it comes to the texts listed above, and several will speak in my story. Rogers, for example, makes clear the truth of the misinterpretations. "None of these texts is about Jesus, nor do they include any of his words. Nonetheless, in the debate on homosexuality, these terms often are taken out of their linguistic, historical, and cultural contexts and used to condemn a whole group of people."[14] To reiterate, none of these texts is about Jesus, nor do they include any of His words. Rogers is talking about living in the spirit and the words of the New Covenant, for which Jesus sacrificed his life.

Chris Greenough,[15] senior lecture in theology and religion at Edge Hill University, adds an interesting perspective to this discussion of Jesus and God's words. "The Bible is often used as a source of authority, but it is misleading to call it "the word of God." In fact, Christianity teaches that the word of God is not scripture, it is Jesus Christ."

Time to add the weight of a different perspective on those Unholy Myths.

To be accurate, many diligent scholars have debunked these myths in many books. I thank them for their dedication to deliberate and factual work. However, as with many important, enlightening books, man does not read them. Scholarly writing, measured and careful, is not popular. Important and relevant, yes, but not popular or well read.

At this point, I see no reason to be kindly or measured to cruel people who have misused Scripture from their positions of power and trust to abuse a group of God's children. The persistent and hurtful smear campaigns among these persons and their legions of followers have caused an unbelievable level of death and pain of soul. My words, supported by those of the thoughtful, intentional scholars, are straightforward. I am tired of the ever-present and abundant supply of mule muffins. I choose not to participate in their continued acceptance.

My words rise from a Christian, me, who is offended by man's treacherous betrayal of trust and of God's word. From my perspective, the spreading of God's misused words is nothing more than busybody tittle tattle from people malevolently minding someone else's business. This practice does not glorify God in any way.

We begin by examining man's intent by considering his "go to" scriptures.

We could call this first example, games one and two of a three-game series: God 2—Satan 0. In his search for some homosexuality, man looked right past the intent of these scriptures. The devil was hosting one grand party that featured his depraved male toys. The God Wannabe ignores the devil's work and strains to see something that is not there. How ironic.

Genesis 19:1-29
Sodom and Gomorrah

This story, a gruesome one, is not related to homosexuality. Lot invites two male strangers, travelers who happened to be angels, into his home, as was the custom of Sodom and neighboring communities. The townsmen took issue with Lot's hospitality and surrounded his house. The men were hostile. They demanded to know, "Where are the men who came to you tonight? Bring them out to us, so that we may know them." They were blatant in their purpose.

To "know them" meant that the men wanted to rape the strangers. Rape was, and still is, the way men sort out who is has the power. Lot stood firm and defended his hospitality, which angered the mob still more. The ugliness heightened. Lot, himself a stranger in Sodom, refused to submit his visitors to the demands of the thugs at his door. Instead, he pushed his two daughters "who have not known a man" into the rape frenzy. When man wants to satisfy his power tool, the Devil's Joystick (DJ), any approachable object will do.

Okay. I am hard pressed to find any homosexuality here, but I do find an abundance of depravity. Rape, even male-male rape, is not homosexuality. The sex act in question does occur between men, but it is not consensual. The depraved intent is rape, violent sexual abuse, man to man. Of course, the God Wannabes insist that we must believe otherwise. We must fall in line and overlook Lot sacrificing his virgin daughters to the feverishly agitated men. So, what the fabricators of this myth contend is: There is a homosexual needle in this haystack of depraved men who seek immediate sexual satisfaction with the angels. We must ignore the obvious and find that needle!

It seems to me that man should clearly see that the blatant sin before us in Sodom and Gomorrah is the abomination of full-on gross depravity, man's lust for sex with the men inside the home, the visiting angels, and the heinous abuse of Lot's daughters. He does not, however. Man's goal is to discover any Scripture that will allow him to punish homosexuals.

To my way of thinking, the Christians who seek to make this Scripture about homosexuality and to ignore the depravity of the mob subscribe to an unbelievable perversion of their own. Lot joined into the donnybrook to protect his house guest and willingly sacrificed his daughters to the viciousness of the thugs. To ignore the lust and the depravity is, to me, an unnaturalness of a special kind. The frustration of man's immoral, desperate search for proof that what he believes he sees, homosexual-activity, must be as intense as the thug's urgency to rape.

One other observation. Scripture says that one of the sins of Sodom and Gomorrah was the inhospitable attitude toward the strangers. The lust to rape the visitors certainly seems embarrassingly inhospitable and pertinent to Scripture. Man overlooked that blatant violation of God's will. God did not overlook it, however.

From the beginning of time, man's "manhood," anatomically named "penis," has been of paramount importance to him. Through this appendage, the first power tool known to man, he wields control over women and humiliates the men whom he has, for instance, already bested in battle. Rape is, for him, the manly display of dominance. Nothing about this has changed.

His manhood is so important that he often names the appendage and the attached testicles, and he visits them, recreationally, from time to time. Too much information? Perhaps. Nevertheless, it is a significant piece of the whole of man's story. I know this from my research and from my 20 years as the invisible female journalist. While the job supported my family, it also exposed my sensibilities to an extraordinary level of crass comments and behaviors of the alpha males among my colleagues and the men, men of prominence and power, on my beat.

When we admit it, we women know, as did Lot's daughters and the women in Gibeah, that women are expendable when it comes to satisfying the needs of man's power tool. Man's sense of entitlement comes through his fraudulent headship. A headship that he determined for himself and for the needs of his power tool are of overriding importance.

As women, we also know that man will blame us for his impulses, just as man excuses the moral corruption in Sodom and blamed the female Adam for his disobedience to God in the Garden of Eden.

We are, to this day, aware and wary of men who have demonstrated or voiced their possible aggression. Men are strong, and their power tool is always only a thought away from action. I can attest to this truth. As I was editing copy for the day's edition, my boss stood next to me, nattering and being annoying. In the corner of my vision, I could see he was aroused. He shoved his hands in his pockets and hurried off to his boss's office. If he could do this in the middle of the office, I perceived this as a warning that he might try even more if we were alone. I made sure that never happened.

What has this to do with man's disregard for the lesson in Ruth? Everything.

God, in writing the story of Ruth and the anointing of same-sex relationships, made clear a significant point: man is not the be-all and end-all in every story, every situation. In the Book of Ruth, Boaz, the man of the hour, is unceremoniously dismissed from the action as soon as he impregnates Ruth. This act destroys man's contention that he is essential to everything. Boaz's job was to redeem and to impregnate Ruth.

I suspect, though I cannot know for sure, that God gave man the adored appendage for two basic purposes: convenient procreation and convenient urination during his hunting, gathering, and warring. To rape is man's decision and is not part of God's plan. To rape does not bring glory to God; it celebrates man's allegiance himself and to Satan.

Man's foolish interpretation of Sodom and Gomorrah shows that the God Wannabes not only are marvelous myth writers, but they also are championship conclusion jumpers. If we have male-male raw sex brewing, and "strange flesh" in the mix, surely, homosexuals must be involved.

The group dedicated to persecuting homosexuals loves to use the stories of Sodom and Gomorrah in defense of their position against the undesirables. The scriptures send chills up their spines. And they snarl "Sodom and Gomorrah! Sodom and Gomorrah!" when they cut their eyes and condemn homosexuals. Only their misinterpretations of Leviticus titillate them more than the outrageous abuses in Sodom and Gomorrah.

Romell Parks-Weekly,[16] a Bible scholar and writer for AffirmingTheology.org, writes this, "Let me state this plainly. Bestiality was the sexual sin of the Sodomites, not homosexuality. God destroyed them for precisely the same reason He destroyed the world during the days of Noah. They were a wicked people and they committed abominations, pursuing sexual activity with angelic beings (beings of an other created kind.)"

Today's Christians, with unwavering allegiance to their misinterpretation of Sodom and Gomorrah, would do well to read Ezekiel 16:49-50, in which God explains His reason for destroying Sodom. "Now this was the sin of your sister Sodom: She and her daughters were arrogant, over fed and unconcerned; they did not help the poor and needy. They were haughty and did detestable things before me. Therefore, I did away with them as you have seen." To paraphrase, God turned the city to rubble and ashes because of pride, an overabundance of food, gross idleness and indifference to the poor and the needy, haughtiness, and other detestable abominations, like rape. Not homosexuality, as the God Wannabes contend.

For emphasis, homosexuality, was not even a word when Sodom and Gomorrah fell.

I believe that it is important, too, that we include the leadup to the destruction. In Genesis 18:16-33, "The LORD was walking with Abraham and some other men and talking about what God was planning to do about Sodom and the other cities." In verses 23 and 24, Abraham came near and said, "Will You indeed sweep away the righteous with the wicked? Suppose there are fifty righteous with the wicked who are in it? Will You indeed sweep it away and not spare the place for the sake of the fifty righteous who are in it?" Abraham persisted with his questions, and the LORD continued to say that He would not sweep the city away, even if there were only 10 righteous among the wicked.

Abraham and the LORD went their separate ways.

God had withheld from Abraham His annoyance with the deafening outcries to Him about the wickedness in these cities. In His earthly investigation of Sodom and Gomorrah, God found not a single righteous person among their inhabitants, and He made fiery history out of Satan's rampant wickedness in those cities.

The events that led to the rape scene and the eventual destruction of these offending cities had nothing to do with homosexuality. God found the wickedness that He sought long before the Christians fabricated their "sinful" homosexuals. God prevailed then. He likely will prevail again.

One other point, as I considered the truth of what really happened in Sodom and Gomorrah, I laughed. While the God Wannabes were so intent upon exposing their ignorance of homosexual activity, they didn't realize that the thugs were behaving in the thrall of Satan himself. The devil was controlling man's power tool, which I sarcastically call the "Devil's Joystick (DJ)." Man's displeasure and despicable behavior are, after all, a game to Satan.

The men of Sodom were so intent upon raping someone, the devil just grabbed hold of their urgency and whipped those thugs around in a frenzy. The abomination that the homosexual seekers sought lay within themselves, as willing voyeurs, in the service of the Satan at play. The behavior of the men in Sodom and Gomorrah is not God-like. Neither is ignoring that behavior in pursuit of a scapegoat.

Now, given our observations, I think that we may conclude that the abominations also lie within the blatant misuse of Scripture.

Basically, the God Wannabes are telling us to ignore man's service to the devil and to find those loathsome, threatening homosexuals. Don't judge my behavior; Go after the real sinners. An example of the God Wannabes' finest misdirection.

Judges 19:1-30

We can call this one: Game 3 of the series. Again, man strikes out, and the score is God 1—Satan 0. God called the game on account of an abundance of abominations.

The story in Judges is similar to that of Sodom, but even more revolting in its depravity. Again, strangers are housed, this time in Gibeah. Again, the men of the city came and demanded the right to rape the visitor. The human message in this case, say the scholars, is about retaining male dominance, which I mentioned in the last chapter. Male over male and, always, male over female. Once again, the women are sacrificed for the males who were secured in the home.

This Biblical message here, too, is that God considers the city's grievous sins as the deplorable acts of greed, injustice, inhospitality, excess wealth, indifference to the poor, and general wickedness.

The irony of the God Wannabes wanton disregard for truth in search of non-existent homosexual activity is appalling and another misuse of Scripture. The thugs from the city came and demanded "Bring out the man who came to your house so we can have sex with him." (Judges 19:22 NIV) The KJV uses the more refined ". . . that we may know him." Man again fails to see the violent difference between consensual sex and rape. Nevertheless, he remains titillated by the violence and the expectation that homosexual activity will show itself.

The God Wannabes really pile up the mule muffins in their intense need to find homosexuality in these verses, and the slumgullion is vile. You can smell it.

Short version of Judges 19:23-24: A man traveling with his

concubine finds the customary shelter in the home of an old man in Gibeah. The thugs show up and demand that the host send out the man. Oh, my, no says the host. "No, my friends, don't be so vile. Since this man is my guest, don't do this outrageous thing. Look, here is my virgin daughter, and his concubine. I will bring them out to you now, and you can use them and do to them whatever you wish. But as for this man, don't do such an outrageous thing."

As with the host in Sodom, the man pushed his maiden daughter into the clutches of the enraged thugs. (I doubt that she was eager to go.) The thugs persisted in their demand. One female sacrifice was not enough. The traveler pushed out his concubine, whom the thugs raped throughout the night. The woman dragged herself to the doorstep where she died. The man found her in the morning and slung her body over his donkey. "When he reached home, he took a knife and cut up his concubine, limb by limb, into twelve pieces and sent them into all the areas of Israel." (Judges 19: 29)

Somehow, the God Wannabes are so stimulated by their search for their mythical abomination, that they failed to hear Satan whispering in their ears. In their misuse of Scripture, they missed the monstrous depravity of the rape-unto-death scene to find evidence of "The homosexuals! The homosexuals!" This seems an egregious perversion of decency—an abomination—beyond description.

Again, Satan grabbed the multitude of DJs and whipped those boys into a frenzy. He didn't let go of their DJs until the men had raped the woman to death. And, still, the God Wannabes hold tight to their myths about the sinfulness and the perversion of the "homosexuals" in Sodom, Gomorrah, and Gibeah. Tell me again about how the God Wannabes are working for the glory of God.

Hmm. Perhaps Satan and man's DJ fetish continue to have a hand in today's misuse of Scripture. Oh, but in the name of God, of course.

Leviticus 18:1-30
Leviticus 20:1-27

In using these scriptures to support their theory, the God Wannabes achieved an abomination of mythical proportion for sure.

Leviticus, their proof that God finds homosexuality repugnant is, in fact, no proof at all. In truth, Leviticus is about the purity of Jews over Gentiles and the Holiness Code of Leviticus.

Daniel A. Helminiak, PhD,[17] in *What the Bible Really Says About Homosexuality*, writes that the "Holiness Code of Leviticus prohibits male same-sex acts for religious reasons, not for sexual reasons. The concern is to keep Israel distinct from the Gentiles." In short, the violation is of Old Testament laws that protect Jewish purity, not the male-to-male sex. Abomination, as it appears in Leviticus and the Holiness Code, is the equivalent of being ritually unclean, a big taboo in Jewish culture in those times.

Abomination is not the big, hairy, scary calling out of homosexuality that the questionable Men of God would have it be. Nevertheless, it is tough to shout, "You are ritually unclean!" when you wish to ridicule someone. Although true words in the days of Moses, they don't carry the same punch as "You are an abomination to the LORD!"

Here's another disparaging note for those pernicious mule-muffin sellers. The Rev. Dr. Nancy Wilson[18] in *Outing the Bible* says, "The term abomination was a very specific word that referred to idolatry, not literally to sexual sins." If I understand correctly, the idolatry would be the love of money and possessions, man considering himself better than the poor man, man's adoration of his power tool, and the inordinate attention to all of the other things mentioned before. No matter. The self-appointed God Wannabes will not be deterred by fact.

Helminiak[19] also draws attention to the cultural differences between the days of ancient Israel and today's culture. "Except for unusual circumstances," he says, "Sex has no implications for religious identity. No sex today, gay or straight, has the religious association to which Leviticus objected. So, the Leviticus Code is irrelevant in deciding whether gay sex is wrong."

According to the scholars, the Holiness Code and any reference to same-sex activity has to do with maintaining the male gender superiority. Man is the penetrator, the superior one. If he allows himself to be penetrated, then he has fallen to the status of woman. Maintaining the patriarchal society was of paramount concern and remains so today.

Furthermore, I reiterate here that the word homosexual is not a word the ancients would have known, understood, or cared about. This is a fact that should not be easily dismissed. Today's tensions between the sexual taboos in Leviticus and man's pursuit of homosexuals is wholly the construct of man for his own purposes. God is not involved in this tug of-war or in the unwarranted persecution of His children.

Rogers adds a note of finality. "When these texts in Leviticus are taken out of their historical and cultural context and applied to the faithful, God-worshipping Christians who are homosexual, it does violence to them." [20]

1 Corinthians 6:9-17
1 Timothy 1:3-13

Homosexual in these scriptures has to do with the incorrect translation that was picked up from the first edition of the RSV in 1946. The word homosexual has been inappropriately included in lists in 1 Corinthians and 1 Timothy. Because the lists provide no context for the words in them, scholars conclude that it is difficult to know exactly what they mean.

This ambiguity does not matter to our God Wannabes. Their uninformed assertions are intended to keep the men relevant and to stir rancor among their followers. How and where the word appears or whether anyone understands the list is irrelevant. With man's regrettable and biased insertion of that one modern word in ancient text and the blatant rewriting of Leviticus, the

God Wannabes can point to the Bible and proclaim, in truth, that "It's in the Bible! Here! See it for yourself!" By their will they have solidified the misinformation.

Well, I believe we have added substantial weight to the wings of the Unholy Myths. You can be sure that the God Wannabes will not relent. Promoting prejudice is their bread-and-butter. The rules and the authority in the Old Testament sell; The New Testament messages of love, equality, freedom of choice, and living a joyful life lack the conviction of those hardline Old Testament rules.

You know, before we end this chapter, I think we need to give man, Satan, and the DJs a little more consideration. As I sit here, thinking through man's myths, and how man continues to push his spurious claims to support his beliefs, I see a pattern.

None of this censure of homosexuals has anything to do with God. Instead of glorifying God with his deeds and his behavior, man glorifies himself and his libidinous lust. That man recorded any of this in any Bible attests to the prominence of this self-interest. Just give the idea some thought as you sit in your comfortable reading space.

Since the beginning of time, man's attention has been consumed by the needs of his manhood and the feeling of raw power that emanates from its ownership. I know that this is a blunt statement. However, I, like many of us through history, have foolishly fallen into pattern of accepting man's justification to denounce homosexuals because of his interest in his own dominance.

After all, they say, it's in the Bible. Part of the Leviticus Holiness Code is devoted to maintaining the purity of man's place in society. Leviticus is specific. The Scripture is about a man maintaining his place in the hierarchy of man by avoiding penetration. A man penetrated by another man reduces him to the emotional and societal status of a woman. Man's fear for his literal manhood shapes his decisions. Based upon my years of experience amid some of the more-vulgar among men and observing man's not-so-subtle behaviors, I shall not qualify my words.

To further meet the needs of his adored power tool, he routinely risked the life of another man, a eunuch, or a loyal servant, by taking him into battle to serve his pressing sexual needs. Sodom, Gomorrah, and Gibeah were all about man's driving need to rape, which man did with consuming satisfaction. Not to put too fine a point on man's misinterpretation of Scripture, man's service to his DJ and to Satan are habits that have been accepted, excused, and refined over time.

Next, is the word *homosexual* in the Bible?

Does the Word Homosexual Appear in the Bible?

T he answer to the question above is yes, but not until 1946, when the panel of learned men erroneously added it to the new Revised Standard Version (RSV) of the Bible. However, although the topic is a notable one, I believe that is the wrong question to ask. In my view, we should ask a different question, such as, why is the19th century word in ancient Scripture? Man controls every word written about the Bible. He started this nonsense. Why?

Why is man so single-minded about proving that God was wrong in creating two things: an equal partnership between Adam and Eve and the offending homosexuals? Perhaps we can determine some reasonable premise for His actions.

Some of my statements are sure to rile your thinking.

Since the of the creation of the male Adam and the female Adam from "Our" image, two bits of information have been true. First, the male Adam has persistently sought support for his notion that he is bigger and more important than the female Adam. We covered that hot topic in Chapter 1. Second, man has feverishly sought support for his contention that God abhors the group of His children who are homosexual. Man has labeled them "an abomination to the Lord."

At least since 1909, when the word homosexual surfaced in the United States, man has used that word to demean, vilify, and persecute these among God's children. Man does not understand these children and chooses to remain willfully ignorant of them. His ignorance invigorates his unwarranted pursuit of homosexuals.

Even though the Germans are credited with coining the word, they did not add that word to Leviticus until 1983. Curiously, that was the same time when *homosexual* was spontaneously included in some of our bibles. And, yes, there is a story behind this.

The addition of the word coincided with two situations: the increasingly contentious political environment in the United States in the 70s and 80s, and the reprinting of the German Bible in 1983. Although Bible scholars contend that the addition of the word lacked credibility, the act, nonetheless, opened the door to further corruption of Scripture.

Currently, Leviticus 18:22 says, "Thou shalt not lie with mankind, as with womankind: it is abomination." Contrary to man's titillating belief, the earlier text was not about male-to-male sexual encounters. Instead, that Scripture was among long-standing taboos, such as maintaining purity between Jews and Gentiles. Jews considered themselves a pure people. Gentiles not so much. The Leviticus Holiness Code laid the groundwork for the intent of the Scripture.

Until 1868, male-to-male sex was simply a normal part of life, as is well recorded in history. In Cicero's time, for instance, men were free to have sex with other men. Acceptable partners were slaves, male prostitutes, and entertainers. Generally, speaking, though, the men preferred boys between the ages of 12 and 20.

The Leviticus text began quite differently from its current version. The first German Bible, published in 1522 reads: "Man shall not lie with young boys as he does with women, for it is an abomination."[21] Ed Oxford learned that earlier bibles from around the world, also contained that translation. For example, Martin Luther's Bible, in original German and published in 1545, uses the words boy molesters. Pederasty, pedophilia, was the object of scorn in Leviticus.

In full disclosure, I researched some materials about 1 Corinthians 1: 19-20 in bibles published before 1946. (Online versions of the bibles and specific Scriptures are a boon to mankind.) The word homosexual does not appear in any of them. This does not surprise me. As I have said before, the word was coined in Germany in 1868, which makes it improbable that homosexual should have appeared in any Bible published before that time. So, if man says otherwise, he is creating his own versions of Scripture.

There is nothing mystical or obscure about what I write here. You can know everything I know by asking questions and continuing to ask questions until you find an understandable answer. I have asked these questions for you and supplied the sources for my answers. Because 21st century technology makes finding answers so easy, it also makes doubly annoying man's willful ignorance of what the Bible does say.

I also found materials by men who assert several contradictions to sources from which I have gathered the information. I mention this because when you research for yourself, you will encounter them. They contend, for instance, that pederasty is not a topic in any Greek translation, and that homosexuals are condemned. Well, not a sliver of the evidence supports their assertions. Their research is limited and shortsighted.

Here's the backstory on the change in the Leviticus text that I learned from Oxford: For economic reasons, when the Germans published their new Bible in 1983, they hired the American publishing house, Biblica.[22] To help the Germans, Biblica paid to produce the new version. Interestingly, Biblica also is the publisher of record for the notorious New International Version (NIV) of the Bible, the one that had wrongly included homosexual. Inexplicably, homosexuality replaced the pederasty reference in the new Bible. I found no reference to any panel making an informed decision about changing the Leviticus text.

Twentieth century man, so obsessed was he with homosexuality, he deliberately inserted the 19th century Anno Domini

(AD) word, homosexual, to the ancient Before Christ (BCE) text. It remains unclear whether the Germans authorized the American publisher to change the text in their bibles. However, the word appeared in their new Bible and in ours. Also, coincidentally, this was the time when the vilification of homosexuals was gaining public momentum.

The questionable addition in Leviticus does not clarify when man created boogeymen of homosexuals, who existed long before the damning adjective/noun was coined. By extrapolating unintended meanings from pieces of select Scripture, man turned his fallacious interpretations to his advantage. His decision to remain willfully ignorant of the Scripture's historical and cultural meaning has aided his censure. This willful ignorance also allowed man to casually divert attention from his fondness for his manhood to the unwanted and so annoying homosexual.

I fully expect that man will present, in his defense against my statement, more of his literal interpretations of Scripture, not actual words from God, to prove that his line of argument is correct. Some habits are tough to break.

I interrupt my narrative here because the trajectory of life for homosexuals has been dramatically altered by the error of translation from Greek to English.[23] I have not included the actual translation because, unless one is knowledgeable of the Greek language, the explanation is a distraction. It is enough to know that the inclusion is considered incompetent and in error. However, I believe the information about the incorrect translation in 1946 is important to the understanding of how man has granted himself unfettered license to persecute homosexuals.

Oxford and his research partner, Kathy Baldock, learned that the publishing faux pas resulted when the 22-man translation team for the Revised Standard Version of the Bible (RSV) wrongly accepted the incorrect translation that joined two Greek words to create the English word homosexual. That error appeared in the first edition of the RSV in 1946, and the insertion of the word into a list of "unacceptable behaviors" in 1 Corinthians (later in 1 Timothy) energized man's bigotry. The list is vague and without foundation, say scholars.

(For reference, the RSV team and publishers were working to create a version of the Bible that was more readable and accessible in its updated language. The team based its work mainly upon the King James Version KJV (1611), the English Standard Version ESV (1885), and the American Standard Version ASV (1901).

After the revision was published, a young seminarian scrutinized the contents of the RSV Bible. He called out the learned men and persuaded them that the translation was incorrect. Homosexual should not have been included in the text of 1 Corinthians. The translation team revisited the evidence and agreed. However, the revised edition had been published, and the error was anchored in text for the next 10 years. The publishing contract specified that the team would not propose any alterations to the RSV during those years.

The sweet smell of vindication for their views, however short lived it should have been, reawakened the men who revile those whom they do not understand. The information revitalized the numerous, equally vindictive, gossip-mongering teams of followers. In the 77 years since that error, the bigoted group of God's children, the God Wannabes, has given itself the right to hold those others accountable for being sin incarnate. Until then, those who were engaged in same-sex relationships had been living peacefully, as God had intended.

Man discovered that, in addition to the RSV translators, other translation teams had been working on renewed publications of the first editions of the New American Standard Bible (NAS), The Living Bible (TLB), and the New International Version (NIV). Presumably, those teams missed the notification that the error had been removed from subsequent publications of the RSV. To the misfortune of homosexuals, the condemning word remains in many bibles. The word will remain in those bibles to perpetuity, unless, of course, the spirit of just and honorable stewardship of God's word is realized and acted upon. However, I am sure that you may have heard of the possibility of hell freezing over.

The incorrect inclusion of that word in the RSV Bible has resulted in untold deaths, physical and emotional pain, and unnecessary, painful separation from God among homosexuals. Although the error was withdrawn in the subsequent publication of the RSV Bible, and researchers announced their actions, the "justified" attack on homosexuals was engaged. Man can now say, "It's there! It's right there for us to use!" Yes, the word is in the Bible. Man made sure it would be.

Other bible publishers picked up the error, and the impact of the word's erroneous inclusion in the RSV will live on in infamy. So long as man continues to play God, the hate and the prejudice resulting from that error in judgment will continue to spread, unabated.

So, the answer to the title question is: Yes, homosexual is there, but as a shameful mistake. Man makes much ado about this inclusion. God says nothing in His own words about it.

Daniel A. Helminiak makes some important points in *What the Bible Really Says about Homosexuality*. "Research shows that the Bible is basically indifferent to homosexuality in itself. The Bible is concerned, as with heterosexuality, only when practices violate other moral requirements."[24] Those would be the practices of rape and other abuses in the translations of Sodom and Gomorrah. Helminiak adds, "Nonetheless, biblical teaching is an important basis for Judeo-Christian beliefs. And every opinion, religious or otherwise, should rest on fact."[25]

Jack Rogers offers a broader perspective. "It is clear that Jesus did not see humanity as universally heterosexual. Jesus recognized and acknowledged many types of sexual difference, even a society in which such differences would have been downplayed, hidden, or even punished."[26] Rogers speaks about Matthew 19:20: "For there are eunuchs who were born thus from their mother's womb, and there are eunuchs who were made eunuchs by men, and there are eunuchs who have made themselves eunuchs for the kingdom of heaven's sake. He who is able to accept it, let him accept it." (NKJV)

In 1983, some unnamed man intentionally entered *homosexual* into Leviticus, which changed the meaning of the original text to match man's incorrect literal interpretation of that Scripture. As though the inclusion of the 19th century word in 1 Corinthians and 1 Timothy was not a big enough insult to God's Word, man continued to change Scripture to suit himself.

Biblegateway.com shows Leviticus 20:13 as the verse of record with this 19th-century distortion of the Holiness Code. "If a man practices homosexuality, having sex with another man as with a woman, both men have committed a detestable act. They must both be put to death, for they are guilty of a capital offense."

You know, the addition of the 19th century word to the ancient text to get one's way is so preposterous, so self-serving and vindictive, as to be the height of ridiculousness. Moses, who translators say wrote Leviticus, did not have the word *homosexual* in his lexicon. However, a more-current man, in his ignorance and lust for power, used it. Adding homosexuality to the ancient text is as disrespectful and absurd as an arrogant beginning art student boldly desecrating the Mona Lisa with a touch of modern-day lip color. But man is not averse to disrespect.

Further comments on Leviticus say that Leviticus 20:13, without the incorrect word, was initiated to address the threat of a specific ancient Greek practice of pederasty and was not intended as an outright ban on male homosexuality. As a matter of reference and understanding of the term, the Holy Roman Catholic Church's attachment to the Old Testament and pederasty, the sexual activity involving a man and a boy or youth, is well recorded. The penchant for the abominable practice has continued for centuries. It also has been studiously ignored.

Most notably, when Pope Benedict died, he was lionized for

his scholarship and his writings and his leadership in the church. Yes, he may have excelled in scholarship. And I can understand the newscasters not mentioning his role in perpetuating the practice of pederasty. The print media took a different tack. The print news focused Pope Francis's criticism that Pope Benedict's death being instrumentalized (sic), a tool for people to score "points." It seems to me that the men who suffered from Pope Benedict's failure to censure and to remove the priests who practiced pederasty from their home parishes might call the reports sanitized.

Given man's allegiance to Satan and to the Devil's Joystick, it is possible, if not probable, more examples of male God Wannabes will be added to the infamy. Man's attention to the needs of his DJ is ubiquitous.

By the way, science says that pederasty has nothing to do with homosexuality. Pederasty is a vexation unto itself, and the one should not be compared to or confused with the other.

Rogers put a finer point on this discussion. "When we interpret Scripture in a way that is hurtful to people, be sure that we are not glorifying God. 'You will know them by their fruits' was Jesus' criterion for judging false prophets. (Matt. 7:16) Whether our interpretations of Scripture result in love of God and neighbor is a practical test of whether our interpretation is incorrect."[27]

Okay. Take a step back. I almost sent us down the prescribed education pattern of learning. You know. The instructor, in this case man, sets the parameters of the discussion, and we students of his word merrily chase off after his premise. I have allowed us to be sucked into man's vortex of swirling words that give us answers to the wrong questions. However, as an ordinary person who is trying her best to fulfill God's calling, I have had enough mule muffins soaked in bilge water to last a lifetime. Yes, I am darned agitated about the rewriting of Leviticus and our unswerving pursuit of accepting man's premise that we should consider Leviticus useful at all.

Man has indeed tinkered with the text from as long ago as the 1500s. Yes, man changed the intent of that Scripture from condemning pederasty to condemning homosexuality. Why? Because man needed a scapegoat, a plausible explanation for his dogged pursuit of homosexuals. His knickers were knotted because male-to-male sex, which had been part of life, all life, from its beginning, now had a name, and it became a scary thing. Who cares? I shout that question in frustration and disbelief and add that the pursuit of this information is little more than another of man's efforts to distract us from the truth. God determined the answer to man's pursuit of Leviticus with His declarations of *everything* and *all* in Genesis.

Moreover, Christ died on the cross to consecrate the New Covenant, the New Testament. The new covenant was to be the guide for Christian life from that day forward. The Old Testament became old news. The New Testament was presented as the plan for a life of love, free choice, and acceptance, based upon one's relationship with God and His son, Jesus. Christ's death satisfied the laws of the Old Testament. The blood of Christ washed away our sins. We are all one in Christ. All of which makes Leviticus a book of history. It is a record that we can review to help us consider the mercies that have changed our lives. Leviticus has nothing to do with the here and the now.

For many, the past is a panacea, an elixir, that eases their perceived unpleasantries of today. And that's okay. We can live in whatever stage of life that suits. The trouble is man betrays the trust that his followers have in him as an authority figure. In his propensity to preach from the books of yesterday, he betrays that trust and wreaks untold havoc on that steadfast trust.

God said that He made everything, from the smallest of creatures to the greatest. And that everything He made was not only good, but also very good. This includes homosexuals. No matter how much man twists Scripture to declare otherwise.

To underscore that bit of His greatness, He declares in Galatians 3:28 that we are all one in Christ. There are no separations of class or gender or bondage, or any other contrivance of separation. We are equal in God's sight.

"God said" trumps all of man's lame literal interpretations of Scripture.

Or, as a man of God do you believe and teach only that which suits your purposes? Have you read the Third Commandment about misusing God's name?

∽

We have talked about the wrongly conceived intellectual reasons for man's focus on his headship, however impertinent the goal may be, and on homosexuality. I, for one, am choking on the diversionary servings of mule muffins to distract us from man's spurious intentions. Based upon my research for this nonfiction story, I discerned a well-recorded pattern.

From this pattern, I have concluded that man's fixation on homosexuality lies with two distinct possibilities, if not probabilities: his willful ignorance of homosexuality coupled with his fetishism of his manhood. I have dubbed man's first power tool the Devil's Joystick (DJ). Man has other names for his rechargeable power tool, things like Thor or Big Man or Mr. Happy and the boys, but I prefer mine. It speaks to the truth of how it fits into the man's history and his disrespect for God. I also think it suits God's thinking, too. Proverbs 23:7 summarizes that thought best: As he (man) thinks in his heart so is he." I do believe that He might be more than a little miffed at man's rewriting of Leviticus 18:22 to suit his needs and those of Satan.

I suspect, too, that you bristle at the thought that any of the God Wannabees is working for Satan. Answer me this: If man is doing anything that works against God's love and does not glorify God with his actions, for whom is man working? How do you see it?

In further evidence of his preoccupation with his manhood, man has recorded his fondness for satisfying his power tool. For instance, in biblical times, man, probably the ranking leadership, would risk the life of a eunuch or a servant during his warring adventures to satisfy his sexual needs.[28]

Man perverted Scripture still more when he ignored the truth of the violent rape scenes in Sodom, Gomorrah, and Gibeah. He presented, without fact, that those abominations are demonstrations of rampant homosexuality. Rape puts man in service to the devil and blinds him to see Scripture in its full horror. God does not condone rape, and I think it safe to say that He is offended by the misuse of His words from Scripture. To say that rape is something other than rape certainly must be a sin.

By chance, have you noticed the dichotomy between what man has written about the destruction of Sodom and Gomorrah, as God's prophesy in Genesis, and what God said in his conversation with Abraham in Ezekiel? God said then that He destroyed Sodom and the other cities because of their abominations of gluttony, greed, and inhospitality. The authors of those books wrote about the abomination of man's intense need to satisfy the overwhelming urge of his power tool. I guess the reader could extrapolate God's meaning from the raging depravity, but the scribe's vivid recounting of the violence does not bring the abominations to mind. The men certainly are inhospitable, though.

In other Scripture, scholars say, man believes that he must be the penetrator because to be penetrated reduces him to the status of the lowly woman, he loses his place in the male hierarchy. In short, in his obsession with his manhood, he is equally worried about being emasculated by another idolater.

It seems that the appendage God gave man as a matter of practicality (convenience for procreation and urination during his hunting, gathering, and warring), became Satan's toy of choice in Sodom, Gomorrah, and Gibeah. Satan transformed man's obsession with his power tool into the Devil's Joystick, by which he led the men into an evil frenzy. Before you fall into a snit, read on to the vivid lessons in God's word.

Beginning with the Leviticus Holiness Code, particularly the original Leviticus 18:20, man is rebuked for his penchant for pederasty, the practice of man taking sexual pleasure with boys and young men. This usually happened in the temples. What better place for Satan to flout his control over man to taunt God but in the temple? The men certainly were up for it. The practice of pederasty was so prevalent and accepted that many fathers sent their sons to be sexual acolytes, hoping that their boys would find favor with some well-established older man.[29] Satan was happy; Leviticus was not. Hence the words in the earlier translation 18:20, "Man shall not lie with young boys as he does with women, for it is an abomination."

Moving on to Sodom, Gomorrah, and the lesser-known-but-more-disgusting Gibeah in Judges, we have Satan in full control of the Devil's Joystick. The needs of the DJ must be satisfied, but not just man-to-angel, as recorded in Sodom and Gomorrah.

Man idolizes his manhood, and he pays much attention to it. I say this without fear of contradiction. In addition to recorded history, 25 years of marriage, and 20 years of work in a man's world, support my statement. And I believe, without hesitation or reservation, that any female reader of this story could add countless examples of man's idolatry.

For instance, history records decades, in the 15th and the 16th centuries, during which man wore a codpiece, with great pride.[30] A codpiece is a pouch that attaches to man's breeches and cradles his manhood with prominence in public. The men went to great lengths to decorate their codpieces so that each was more flamboyant and more interesting than another man's codpiece. Now, if the codpiece is not an example of man's Sodomite moment, his abomination before the Lord, can you offer a more appropriate description?

"That was in another time. We can't look at the codpiece as

a sign of man's obsession." So, you say. Men still buy them and wear them privately. Purveyors of codpieces have some fancy, seductive choices online.

More recently, information online emphasized man obsession with his power tool. Along about the same time as the codpiece fetish, a "penis panic" broke out in Europe.[31] Men believed that witches were stealing penises and hoarding them in birds' nests. They so believed and feared this possibility that they took to their beds in "illness."

In another example, men thought that their penises were shrinking or disappearing. Man so feared the loss of his penis that, "Some try to stall the shrinkage by securing their members with strings or clamps, or by having relatives hold their penises in relays until they get treatment."[32] These references to man's fears are among the milder ones, but I think that the mental pictures vividly underscore man's obsession.

Since that time, many such panics have been recorded. The last one documented is 2013 in Africa. I did not research further. The stories were too farcical to add more to the pile. Nothing was mentioned about a panic among American men. This does not mean, however, that such a panic has not occurred or does not currently terrorize American men. We avoid embarrassing our own with reports of their penis fears and fetishes.

In clearing out the SPAM in my email files, I discovered still other demonstrations of man's obsession. For a fee, a man can purchase pills, potions, and the details of African rituals to make his power tool longer, stronger, and with improved staying power. These products surely attest to his insatiable vanity. As the invisible person in the man's world, I also could recount revolting stories about the immature men who have told about their group contests to show whose power tool is bigger and better. Satan regularly woos man with his seductive siren song.

An example from West Africa in the early part of this century might well be at the heart of man's current fear of homosexuals.

"One boy in Ghana reported that he had gone to fetch water for his father and was returning when [the thief] came behind him, touched him, and immediately he felt his penis shrink until it was no longer visible. Other men reported the same kinds of events. Doctors tried to disabuse these men of their belief." The population became hysterical. At least 36 persons were accused of genital theft and killed. Talk about obsession.

Given how widely men function on hearsay, I think it is reasonable to believe that they, in their willful ignorance, worry that some homosexual will sneak up on them, touch them, and emasculate them.

And if this is not enough to awaken your awareness of man's idolatry of his manhood, consider this: statues all over Europe show male children and men exhibiting their power tools in various stages of function, aberration, and readiness.[34] Yes, they are statues, but the sculptors (all males), felt compelled to glorify the idolatry in three-dimensional replications.

Here are a few things I know from 25 years of marriage and 20 years on the job with men: As a rule, men do not acknowledge their fears about themselves. A man will do just about anything to avoid learning the truth. He cannot remain the macho, macho man if he acknowledges that he remains ignorant on a topic that affects him so distinctly. Truthful information is nearly as toxic to man as Kryptonite is to Superman.

Because he chooses to know virtually nothing about homosexuality and clings to his ignorance, man fears the unknown. Men having sex with men? For crying out loud, he could be next! One of these men might touch him, and who knows what might happen? His manhood might disappear into his abdomen, like the foolish men in history believed. When it comes to his prized appendage, man is not rational. To which the penis panics attest.

So, in his fear, he blames someone else for his emotional discomfort and fear. This time he blames God. Perhaps the individual man does not know, or has not accepted, who he is in Christ.

All of which brings us to the crux of man's need to terrorize homosexuals. Dying on the battlefield is far superior to being raped, emasculated, and demeaned by another man and continue to live.

For centuries, man had no name for male-to-male sexual experiences. It was just what man did. Man fears what he does not understand. Then, man coined a word for this scary thing. What man names, without accurate information on the topic, becomes even more fearsome. The possibility of being called out by or as a homosexual terrorizes him.

The stigma of emasculation is not new. It existed in biblical text. For instance, King Saul so feared Jonathan's relationship with David, the Goliath-slayer, was shaming his son. Saul believed that David's relationship with Jonathan diminished his son's manliness. A king must be manly. If two future kings, Jonathan and David, could succumb to this abomination, how could a mere mortal, resist?

Then, when man found the scary name for a behavior that was normal before the name appeared, man gained incentive to demonize homosexuality and make it God's huge mistake. He entered the word into Scripture to perpetuate his viewpoint. Is it possible that man chooses to remain ignorant about homosexuality? Is it possible that his ignorant belief that a homosexual could take away his manliness keeps him on edge? He fears both the possibility of his power tool shorting out and his being penetrated like a woman. It is best to direct attention away from himself and toward the homosexual.

Come to think of it, he also may be wrestling with his feelings for one of the men in his circle of friends. However, if the Bible and God condemn homosexuality, maybe he can bring enough power to bear to keep them and his thoughts at bay. If God and the Bible say homosexuality is wrong, then he can protest, with the force of the newly written Scripture, against these abominable men and remain macho.

Ironically, I believe this is why man has chosen to ignore the importance of the message in the Book of Ruth and to demean the message about David in Samuel. If God celebrates same-sex relationships in the Bible, then those abominable men are equal to him. Man's belief that he is superior is debunked. Those abominable men have become a threat. Too bad man doesn't understand that gay men lack interest in his manhood.

∽

God woke me from a deep sleep this morning to express some frustration, if not outright anger. Emotion is tough to discern when one has been rudely awakened. If God shouts, I think I heard Him shouting this morning.

"Do they not understand that their idolatry makes them the abomination? Do they not understand that their idolatry takes them away from Me?"

I waited. God remained quiet. I went back to sleep, but not easily.

No, He didn't deliver the text above in one piece, like a Sermon on the Mount. That's a silly thought. He spoke haltingly, in fragments. Like any highly agitated person might. Considering the intensity of energy with which God awakened me and provided His thoughts, I think God is ticked off. I'd say that man's penis-idolatry, his misuse of Scripture, and his unwarranted and deliberate abuse of His homosexual children has God's full attention.

As best that I can, I assure you that I am not making this stuff up. I don't smoke pot, and the only drugs I take are those prescribed by my doctors. I have this to say: As God's scribe of record for this project, it sounds like God is on the edge of another Sodom and Gomorrah moment in time. Or maybe we are experiencing that time already.

With the shouting over, it's time to move on to what Scripture really says.

44

What We Know from the Bible

Before we talk about the Bible and how Scripture supports the fact that God loves all His children, I have some questions. My background is in reporting, editing, and writing. That being the case, questions rise when the information in front of me does not make sense. The current nonsense over homosexuals prompts these questions:

- Where in the Bible, what Scripture, gives any of us the authority to judge any of God's children, God's work, whether we approve or not? We might think the action or the belief is wrong, but what Scripture makes it any of our business? In fact, several Scriptures command or direct against anyone but God exercising judgment. The most prominent of which is Matthew 7:1, Judge not, so that ye are not judged. Then there is James 4:12: There is one lawgiver, who is able to save and to destroy: who art thou that judges another?

- What motivates man to persecute this particular group of God's children with the intensity of a hunter pursuing his prey? I have offered some possibilities.

- As a follower of a God Wannabe, have you ever asked Him, the real God, if you are following the right path? Or do you rely solely upon the man in the pulpit, rather than God?

- Do you know anything about the man of God who has your devoted attention?

- How is it possible for you to work against the God of love? Do you understand that your false statements, even parroted false statements, do that?

- If you are saying unkind things about anyone, even homosexuals, are you honoring the New Covenant and God's painful, sacred sacrifice?

∽

Now, let's see what the Bible has to say about this phony same-sex/homosexual fracas.

Beginning with the beginning, Genesis 1:24-27, here's what we know from the King James Version (KJV):

"And God said, Let the earth bring forth the living creature after his kind, cattle, and creeping thing, and beast of the earth after his kind: and it was so.

"And God made the beast of the earth after his kind, and cattle after their kind, and everything that creepeth upon the earth after his kind: and God saw that it was good.

"And God said, Let Us make man in Our image, after Our likeness: and let them have dominion over the fish of the sea, and over the fowl of the air, and over the cattle, and over all the earth, and over every creeping thing that creepeth upon the earth.

"So, God created man in his own image, in the image of God created he him; male and female created he them."

Now, to this believer, these four verses seem specific. God made everything. All things, great and small. Do you see an, "except for," or "but for," or "other than"? No, neither do I. The words *all* and *everything* are as broad in their scope as they are tight in their meaning. These two words embrace the invisible amoeba that one cannot see with one's own eyes and the elephant that the unaided eye can see from afar. Is there any real need for man to interpret God's words in Genesis? I think not.

Somehow, man overlooked the specifics in verse 26, in which "God said" to get to verse 27 in which the scribe reports on God's word. Based upon my research, "Our image" implies that God is both male and female, which would be a logical view from which to understand that He created both genders. Man holds onto "God created he him," the report, which seems to give man a righteous justification for his "headship" claim. He fails to read the rest of the passage, which says ". . . male and female created he them."

To add a period to those thoughts, in Genesis 1:31, God said that His creation was greater than good. "And God saw everything that he had made, and behold, it was very good . . ." Unlike man's narrow vision and shortsightedness, God sees into eternity and knows all that will come. His vision includes the Book of Ruth, which is key to His long-term and auspicious plan for Naomi and Ruth and for the world.

What more does any of us need to know? God is God and not subject to human thought.

To provide a little historical information about biblical references, in most cases, unless otherwise stated, I have used the New King James Version, which contains more modern language than the original version published in 1611.

Gratefully, the New Testament provides the words of God/ Jesus in red letters to sort the "God said" words of from the black letters in which man shares his limited and primitive opinion of God's intentions. Yes, the apostles had opinions of what God meant, but their words remain opinions and are open to wrongful interpretations. These are man's words, and man has interpreted liberally. No matter how godly the apostles seemed, Jesus rebuked them when they strayed from his teachings. This fact says to me that, regardless of how steeped the men were in the ways of our Lord, they remained fallible men.

What also is true is man's penchant for maintaining his

ignorance and continuing to promote his literal, erroneous interpretations of Scripture. It's convenient to remain ignorant.

∽

Now, returning to the same-sex/homosexuality brouhaha, I'm sure that you have heard the lame quip, "God made Adam and Eve, not Adam and Steve." That viewpoint is quite true in the original creation act. Nonetheless, you forget that God is God. He thinks more broadly and farther ahead than the first person who foolishly uttered those words. In God's plan, today is over before the average man's brain can consider the importance of the moment in which he is living.

Within those two original humans, the female Adam and the male Adam, God planned for the inevitable, the continual change and adaptations among mankind and all His other creations. (I do not use the name Eve here because it was not part of the creation story. Neither was the word apple. Much conjecture exists about the kind of "fruit from the tree of knowledge," but the only time I found an apple depicted in Eden is in a painting by Albrecht Dürer.)

A piece of God's long-range plan is prophesied in the book of Ruth, as it pertains to man's failure to understand or to accept that man is not God. God thought about the evolution of mankind through, to, and long after, the birth of His precious son, Jesus Christ. He instilled genetics into man, and He gave other men the tools to know about genetics at least as far back as the days of Pythagoras, Hippocrates, Aristotle, Epicurus, which was after the time of Moses's writings. The science of genetics has been with us from our beginning. We have expanded our knowledge of genetics with each discovery in each decade. And we gained that knowledge in God's time.

I suspect that God, being the ultimate Creator, thought it would be mundane to lay His hand to ordinariness. So, God built a myriad of subtle changes into mankind's evolution. He didn't want a world full of look-alike Adams. Being an extraordinary Creator, God created a future of continual change and renewal for all His creations.

Thus, if we hark back to the verses in Genesis, God's incredible plan for mankind has resulted in a world currently populated by an estimated 7.9 billion versions of the Adams. Each version is distinctly different from all the others, right down to the identifying marks on our fingertips. He came up with 7.9 billion times 10 of those. Our evolution includes homosexual Adams and heterosexual Adams, both of whom have been with us from the beginning of mankind. In Biblical days, no man got his toga in a twist because of same-sex activity. He had no name for it (that we know of) and frequently participated.

So, what about the Scripture in Leviticus that today's man loves so much, you ask. We attended to that wrongful interpretation in Chapter 3. But, in case you missed the information, Leviticus, until 1983, was about pederasty, pedophilia. Then man arrogantly, deliberately rewrote Scripture to suit himself.

Full disclosure. Ed Oxford, in *"Has Homosexual always been in the Bible?"* [35] says that Leviticus 18:22, as recorded in bibles from around the world, contains the reference to men lying with boys. Martin Luther's Bible, published in 1545, being the most prominent among those bibles. In some versions, Oxford says, these men were called molesters.

However, the KJV, published in 1611, contains the reference to men lying with men. Because I limited my research to easily obtained sources that are available to you, I could find no explanation for why the KJV translation was different from those printed well before any of our contemporary versions were published. The international versions follow the intent of the Leviticus Holiness Code. I can only ask how this bold discrepancy came to be. The translators all started with the same information from the same original-language bibles. This curiosity makes me wonder if this discrepancy is yet another manmade contradiction.

When it comes to the topic of homosexuality, some scholars report that they, too, "struggle" with the notion of homosexuality, how it happens, how to explain it. Especially when the topic involves the story of David and Jonathan. Embracing the idea that those two young men loved each other apparently is beyond their ken.

Surely, these learned men know about science and the properties of evolution. Perhaps these well-educated men are so engaged in the male mystique that they are unable, or afraid, to say honestly and out loud that man has been preaching an inaccurate message for centuries. By man-determined traditions, however, man must never question the sacred bastions of the hierarchy of man and the patriarchy.

If I understand correctly, God doesn't much care whether we know how things happen. He expects us to trust Him and to have faith. He knows how all things work and how they came to be. Thus, we are relieved of the burden of figuring it out.

Homosexuality and heterosexuality are products of genetics, and neither term is mentioned in the Bible. Genetics carry us from one person in our ancestry to the next generation and on to perpetuity. Either you believe that God is capable of greater thinking than you, or you don't.

In 2019, Science magazine reported that there is neither a gay gene nor a straight gene. The article explains the scientific rationale for this conclusion, but, inasmuch as we humans have difficulty understanding the concepts of all and everything in relation to God's plan, I cut to the chase, as they say. ". . . the researchers found that sexuality is polygenic—meaning that hundreds or even thousands of genes make tiny contributions to the trait. That pattern is like other heritable (but complex) characteristics like height or a proclivity toward trying new things."[36]

More importantly, the study demonstrates that one's sexuality, on either side of life's pendulum, is heritable, not a choice. It also means that God did not choose the specific sexuality or qualities thereof for any of His children. He put genetics in motion and let His evolution scheme sort things. He has allowed His plan to evolve into a rich palette of human beings.

Far from being an outcast, Jack Rogers emphasizes the legitimacy of homosexuality with this bit of information. "In 1994, the American Psychiatric Association and the American Psychological Association stated: The research on homosexuality is very clear. Homosexuality is neither mental illness nor moral depravity."[37] This declaration also ended the reign of terror homosexuals had experienced for decades because of man's faulty thinking. Homosexuals no longer were subjected to atrocities such as electric shock therapy, lobotomies with ice picks, and incarceration in institutions for the mentally ill.

The predominately male bastions of psychiatry and psychology also have failed to mention that their decision to remove homosexuality from their official manuals of illnesses resulted from the extensive, careful research, and testing of homosexuals by Dr. Evelyn Hooker.[38] Dr. Hooker, an American psychologist, administered three well-known tests (the names of which are irrelevant to our simple conversation). To ensure that she did not bias the scoring, she secured the services of three world-renown test-evaluation scientists to score the results. The men reported that the results showed, "There was no association between homosexuality and psychological maladjustment."

Hooker's discovery was so groundbreaking that the American Psychological Association recognized her work with the Distinguished Contribution to Psychology in the Public Interest award in 1992. I mention this fact because, prior to Hooker's research, the male-dominated professional-standards groups were sure that their version of the topic was accurate.

Later, those distinguished professional bodies also declared that the two therapies—aversion and conversion—once the "cures" of choice among religious zealots, were no longer considered legitimate treatments. They declared, too, that those therapies are too dangerous to use. Homosexuality comes with the person's humanity and cannot be changed any more than we can change our eye color through therapy. Briefly stated, aversion therapy seeks to persuade the patient that he dislikes sex with his own kind. Conversion therapy seeks to convert the homosexual male into a heterosexual male.

Because *It's Okay to be Gay* is a story of new information, I have added a short explanation of aversion and conversion therapies. Some religious zealots and well-known men of God continue to push for parents to "fix" their gay children. I believe this book will reach enough readers that the information will be passed on diligently. "The Truth about Aversion and Conversion Therapies" will appear at the end of the final chapter. Knowing the truth about these therapies could mean the difference between life and death for the person subjected to that danger.

Everything about us, all of us, has evolved into whatever God intended us to be. Unlike the God Wannabes, I do not think I know so much as God. However, I do trust and believe that, as He said in the beginning, He made everything, without exception.

It is significant to know, too, that homosexual does not appear in any of the myriad of bibles prior to 1946, when the Revised Standard Version (RSV) erroneously included the word homosexual in its publication. The designations of sexuality are facts of life, facts of His creation. They mean no more than saying "man with blue eyes" or "man with brown eyes," specifics that also do not appear in the Bible.

When you check my research, you may encounter some scholars who believe they have unearthed ancient papers that contradict the timing of the word's inclusion. They say certain unpublished papers, which are irrelevant to this story, contradict conventional wisdom. Though the claims may well be true, I focus here on the reliable bibles we can hold or retrieve online.

Regardless of man's many assertions to the contrary, if God made it, then He loves it. It is wholly illogical to believe, even for an instant, that He would make something that displeases Him. Yes, I know. Some God Wannabe will "interpret" a Scripture or three to prove God and me wrong. The men and the women who persist in their relentless persecution of those in same-sex relationships, which are none of their business under any circumstances, have forgotten their fallback platitudes: God doesn't make junk and God doesn't make mistakes. The God Wannabes hold those clichés dear, unless we're talking about something, someone they don't like.

∽

While we are on the topic of genetics, let's consider another of the tried-and-true objections to homosexuality—it's unnatural.

Oh, my. If Christians really subscribe to that absurdity, they must be uneducated and living in primitive shacks on some remote hillside, grunting and using a feral sign language. It seems wholly illogical that they have not witnessed such acts among animals in their lifetimes.

According to my research, the "unnatural" mentioned in Scripture pertains to local cultural opinions about what is considered uncommon in that area, in that time in history, and in that culture. The reference concerns the mores of that area, i.e., how one eats or dresses, social behaviors, that sort of thing, not sexual behaviors.

In the Oxford English Dictionary (OED), the first reference for unnatural is: not in accordance with what usually occurs in nature. The second reference is: not included in nature.

Speaking of the contrary course of nature, as man perceives it, God has created many contradictions to man's perceptions of what is natural and unnatural. I chuckle at man's foolish beliefs, his limited thinking, and his penchant for avoiding the truth of the multitude of God's wonders around him.

God has created so much wonder and so many contradictions to what God Wannabes believe is natural. According to Bruce Bagemihl, a Canadian biologist, he has documented same-sex behavior in more than 450 species of animals worldwide. This same-sex behavior comprises courtship, sexual, pair-bonding, and parental activities, Bagemihl says.[39]

Species of animals that contain homosexual members are as commonplace as cows, horses, wolves, and dogs. More than 450 of God's creations. Think about that for a moment. The thought should bring a sobering moment to the hysteria of "its unnatural." More importantly, that which is in nature parallels man's evolution.

Additionally, many transgender creatures also exist in nature. My favorite is the sweet little clownfish.[40] You know. The little orange-and-white striped fish in the movie, *Finding Nemo*. Anyway, in the life of the clownfish, all begin as males. As they mature, they pair off. The dominant fish becomes female. She mates with the male, and they reproduce. If the female dies, her mate becomes female in order to continue the hierarchy of the school. The hierarchy of the female. Talk about "unnatural" contradictions that should rattle man's certainty about what he knows!

Hold on to your prejudices and misunderstandings for this one. Some female animals can reproduce without mating. The most knowable of these creations is the Komodo dragons, a large, formidable, and dangerous reptile, known to eat small animals and small children. Scientists know that these female dragons can reproduce within themselves.[41] They know this because two dragons have done so in captivity. No males needed.

The California condor[42] is another true wonder among God's creation. Unfertilized condor eggs have produced chicks, through parthenogenesis, reproduction without fertilization. Scientists say that parthenogenesis usually occurs among females that have no access to males. Nonetheless, this published example occurred in two females, both of which had successfully mated with males and produced chicks.

Parthenogenesis is more common in lizards, such as the Komodo dragon, but creation is God's plan and wide open to His determinations.

The final burst of color in God's creative sexual fireworks is the leopard slug,[43] which is a hermaphrodite animal, one that has both male and female sex organs. All leopard slugs can produce offspring. I won't try to explain how they mate. I choose to avoid increasing the angst and the stress you may be experiencing from this new and significantly contradictory information.

Giving in to my sense of impish delight, I add two more examples of God's imaginative and confounding creativity. No sex of any kind is involved.

First is the six-million-year-old geological marvel, the trovant rock.[44] These extraordinary bits of geology, called the living stone, live in Romania. They are a rare phenomenon because they move, they grow, and they reproduce. You homosexual hunters are way too serious about God's functional, imaginative, and joyful creations.

Second is the miracle of the monarch butterfly. This creature begins life as a green caterpillar. To prepare for its transformation, it encases itself in a splendid green cocoon with gold-colored trim. A miracle occurs in that cocoon. The green caterpillar emulsifies into a cocoon full of a yellow goo. Then, over the next few weeks, the molecules in the goo assemble themselves into the beloved orange, black, and white insect called the monarch butterfly.

God is the imaginative Creator supreme. Unlike man's myopic view of his world, God's creativity knows no limits. He can and has created any darn thing He wanted to create and in any form. His creative palette exceeds all explanation, as does His use of it. An hour or two watching Animal Planet, will show how awesome are God's infinite creations.

∞

Let's consider a moment of Christian hubris about their knowledge of homosexuality. You have seen it. Maybe even have experienced it. The righteous critic. The woman with the stern look on her face as she speaks her disapproval of "those people," or the man who holds himself extra straight as he declares, with an air of authority, that another man has, for instance, left his family because he "turned homosexual."

This happened in a recent Bible study. One of the participants stated, with a sharp edge of disdain, that a male friend of hers had "announced that he had turned gay and was leaving his family."

First, it was not her story to tell, and second, because of the science of genetics, her friend did not *turn gay*. No one chooses to be gay, the common term for male homosexuals. Second, the truth is that her friend, a good Christian, finally accepted who he was in Christ. This man had lived an incomplete life in the shadows, living in fear of his Christian friends' reproach, just as this woman had exhibited. Thousands, hundreds of thousands, of human beings live in secret because the good Christians, the God Wannabes, have declared that it is their right to judge and to persecute them in the name of God's righteousness.

Consider this for a moment. Why would anyone, male or female, choose to be gay, knowing that they could be beaten by gay bashers? Or fired from their job? Or thrown out of their rented housing? Or end up in poverty because of man's malevolence? Or be prevented from living a full, godly life in many of the churches that man declares to be God's house?

Moreover, I can think on no good reason why any young person would choose to be abandoned by his Christian parents and forced to live on the streets because he accepted that he was gay and said so. Or thought that he was gay and sought understanding from his family. For that matter, why should any parent live in anguish because someone told them that their child is a sin against God? Do not be deceived by Satan's pure, unadulterated hogwash.

Why would anyone choose to be unwelcome, unwanted in man's so-called House of the Lord, or to live as the man in the story had, afraid to be a real person because Christians have made him afraid? Afraid to be the child whom God created her/him to be? Why?

Perhaps the more significant question is, "Why is it necessary to come out?" I can understand how a young person who is confused would say something, to seek knowledge. But an adult who knows himself or herself? Why is it necessary to make any announcement?

Prejudice and hate against homosexuals are constructs of man. Why encourage his bigotry by deliberately setting yourself apart from the rest of God's children? You are not obligated to explain yourself. What do you do if someone calls you out because they suspect that you are gay? Look them in their eyes and ask, "And your point is?" If they persist, tell them to, "Talk to God. I am not interested." Walk away.

A homosexual child of God is just as important, but no more so, as a heterosexual one. God does not discriminate. Neither did Jesus. Live your gift and tell the fake Christians to pound sand. They can persecute you only to the extent that you allow. Let your authenticity rise proudly above the accusations of the God Wannabes. You have no reason to be or to act ashamed.

Now, let's turn to the Book of Ruth, the story in which God anoints the same-sex relationships that are a vexation to man's spirit.

A Look at the Writing of Ruth

The Book of Ruth, one of only two books in the Bible named for women, is devoted to the deeds and the strengths of two women, Naomi and Ruth. The purpose of the Book of Ruth is, I believe, God's public announcement that same-sex relationships are part of His plan. God knew that man's propensity for self-aggrandizement and maintaining the patriarchy would make the topic of same-sex alliances a lightning rod for abuses of His children. He made clear in this one compact book that same-sex couples are full members of His worldly family. In this case, God demonstrates that Ruth and Naomi are especially important members of His family.

I have used the Amplified Bible for Ruth's story.

As I reported in Chapter 1, my research on The Book of Ruth began after God sat me down in an ill-conceived Bible study of Ruth.[45] The study irritated and offended me because, in many cases, the text of the study strayed from or was not supported by Scripture.

The purpose of the Scripture in Ruth, the studies say, is to show the redemption of Ruth and Naomi. Yes, redemption, right enough. The lawful redemption of the women, Naomi and Ruth, which was the pivotal part of the story, not some earth-shaking spiritual redemption. A closer look at Scripture strengthens my conviction that Ruth is about God's long-range plan in which the lawful, functional redemption of Naomi and Ruth is an integral part of His grand design. God has written His intent for this relationship cleanly and clearly. No frills attached. No additional information needed. No matter how any mortal seeks to alter the intent of God's words.

The thing about words is, they are specific in their meaning, and, used well, they will tell a story so clearly that there is no room for fanciful interpretation.

God wrote the book of Ruth—four chapters, 2563 words (Amplified Bible, AMP)—so cleanly, so economically, and so in the present tense that the reader has no need to create a back-story. Unless, of course, the reader objects to the implication of God's words.

Speaking of contradictions, before I continue with my narrative, I need to clarify some points about how other authors have interpreted the text in Ruth. These next few entries are taken from texts written by female authors, which I have included in my resource list.

The entries are, from my point of view, the authors' personal and traditional expressions of what they believe the Scripture is saying. When you compare these examples with the Scripture in Ruth, it is my firm belief that you will not see a word or a sentence that supports any of their descriptions of Ruth's or of Naomi's behavior. For the sake of space and brevity, I have limited my examples.

- Naomi is ". . . bitter at God, and with two daughters-in-law she wishes would just leave her alone already because she's not in the in-law, let's-have-tea-mood right now."[46]
- "As she urged the girls to return to their homeland, Naomi kicked up her arguments a notch as if to say, The only reason you're following me to Bethlehem is because I'm your only hope for another husband."[47]

- "For instance, as we see in Ruth 3, the act of a man throwing a corner of his garment over a woman symbolized and proclaimed his intent to take her as his bride. . ."[48]

- "In speaking of Boaz's attitude toward Ruth, he was benevolent to . . . the foreigner, the lowly, the poor . . ." and ". . . protecting the innocence of someone he didn't have to notice, much less provide for."[49]

- Ruth was facing ". . . devastating circumstances . . ."[50]

- Ruth ". . . must have felt ill equipped and unable . . ." to do what was expected of her.[51]

If you read such perceptions in the Book of Ruth, send me a note.

As I have said from the beginning of this narrative, God has crafted the story of Ruth and Naomi so well, so tightly that the reader is present with the characters. The reader walks on the dusty road with Naomi and her girls, as Naomi beseeches them to return to their mothers' homes in Moab. The reader sits with Boaz and Ruth, as she takes sustenance at the gleaners table and talks with Boaz and waits in the darkness with Boaz and Ruth, as each shares their understanding of this encounter. She gathers with the elders at the gate of the city while Boaz strikes the deal for the redemption of Naomi and Ruth. Then, she celebrates as the anonymous relative hands his sandal to Boaz.

God wrote Ruth so carefully in "the here and the now" that the reader has no reason to be confused about what is happening or to know more about feelings and expectations. The action unfolds and is not embellished by any useless implications from another time or place.

His words for and about the women are strong, hopeful, positive, and vital. Not a single syllable implies the slightest hint of despair, or discomfort, or fear, or tragedy, or sense of loss among the women. The need for any secondary information is a holdover from man's and woman's misunderstanding. Perhaps, too, man's fear of the true message of these concise chapters of Scripture causes him to embellish the narrative with details that create a suitable story.

The female authors of the studies have relied upon the faulty viewpoint of man's comfortable, convenient, and satisfying interpretation, rather than critically examining the Scripture. Naomi and Ruth are whole and strong, unafraid, purposeful, devoted to each other, and fully in God's care and influence.

During our group discussion, I said, clearly and concisely, that I thought the Book of Ruth appeared to be the anointing of a same-sex relationship. The intake of breath was audible. So was the outrage. That was not what they wanted to hear, and they rejoined the many fantasies embedded in the study. My classmates shunned me in the remaining classes.

I continued to ask how the Scripture supported the study text. For example, I asked in what Scripture does God rebuke Ruth for being a Moabitess? The women replied that I needed to know the background of the Moabites and how the people of Israel mocked them.

I asked, "What words in these scriptures say that I should care about Ruth's background? Scripture refers only to her value as a worker and her association with Naomi. Scripture mentions her city only as identification. The reference bears no more importance than saying, 'Shirley is a Michigander.' No historical references are required to understand God's plainly stated message: Ruth was a woman unto herself and devoted to Naomi." My study mates turned away and looked down at their books.

Turning to Ruth's prominence in the Bible, it seems that God declared, emphatically, by its inclusion in the Bible, that the story of Ruth was of preeminent importance to Him. If God's words about a woman are meaningful enough to write, and to include in the Bible, then He surely must have some meaningful lesson to share.

Because the Book of Ruth has no named author, I consider this a significant indication that God's thoughts about Ruth are paramount. He chose not to select a known author who might be inclined to include his vision of God's intent.

A quote by H.G. Wells, author of *The War of the Worlds*, heightens my belief that God wanted to ensure that He, and He alone, is seen as the author of this book of Scripture: "No passion in the world is equal to the passion to alter someone else's work." As an editor, I know that the temptation to change words or syntax is great. Man's need to edit has been evinced by the many versions of other books in the bibles and of the bibles themselves in print today. Over the centuries, man has reordered Scripture to satisfy his insatiable ego needs. In contrast to the many books with which man has tinkered, the Book of Ruth remains basically unchanged from the story in the first King James Bible.

Other books in both the Old Testament and New Testament also are without specific authors, but the translators for the various versions note a "possible" author, based upon the writing style and time in history. For instance, man credits Moses as the writer of record for much of the Old Testament, and scholars refer to Moses's intent and writing style in speaking about those scriptures. The same is true in the New Testament. Scholars note well the philosophies and the writing styles of the many authors, not the least of which are Matthew, Mark, John, and Paul.

In the case of the Book of Ruth, translators have suggested that Samuel may have written that book. However, they contradict that premise by noting that Samuel probably was dead by the time Ruth was written. So, I repeat the proposition that God is indeed the author of the Book of Ruth.

I suspect, though I cannot prove, that man sees the Book of Ruth as irrelevant to any important thought. After all, Ruth and Naomi were just women. Needy women, which renders the book as hardly worth considering. I also believe that the implication of the content may have skewed man's thinking. Maybe it even disquieted him. It does, after all, speak clearly about a same-sex relationship, the very relationships against which he rants.

Man's prejudices aside, however, God wanted His words and His intent to be as pure as possible. He knew, because God knows everything, that the business of same-sex relationships would one day be a troublesome concept for mankind to embrace. Man is finicky and quite protective of his power and his place in the male hierarchy and in the patriarchy. The Book of Ruth threatens his concept of himself and his place.

Because of His resolve, I believe God selected an unidentified-but-trusted, competent, skillful, worthy scribe who would record, as accurately as possible His narrative of the same-sex relationship between Ruth and Naomi. Unlike the fanciful and modern-day narratives of Ruth, created by the authors of the Bible studies and other commentaries, God describes and carefully lays out a series of clean transactions, without drama or fanciful side issues, that advance His plan.

To begin with, these transactions accomplish His plan of setting up the women to establish the powerful lineage of David, and ultimately, that of Jesus Christ. The transactions among and between the principals are simple: If we do this, then that should happen, assertions that are clear in their intent and in their execution on God's behalf. No love story is implied.

In the Scripture, Naomi is a wise, thoughtful, considerate woman. Ruth loved Naomi and willingly did whatever she must do to care for both of them. She implicitly trusted Naomi and unhesitatingly did what Naomi instructed her to do. Naomi, having lived decades of experiences, knew what must be accomplished and how to go about it.

To God's end, the men in Ruth, although having notable roles, were incidental music to the story of these women. The men came, they took care of their designated business, and, poof, they were gone, without fanfare. Mission accomplished. God gave them no words or inflection of action that suggest they were doing anything more important or more complicated than following the laws of their time. The celebration of accomplishment, that of establishing and caring for the line of humanity to come, lay in the hands of and was demonstrated by Ruth, Naomi, and the women of Bethlehem.

In opposition to the romantic, fanciful study stories that purport to explain Ruth, Scripture is specific to His intent for Ruth. No lollygagging or wooing or seduction appears in God's words.

In some commentaries, the writers refer to the Moabite woman as flawed, or embellish the history behind one disagreeable trait or another, or detail an imaginary wedding. All of which contradicts the simple fact that Boaz married Ruth. This statement in Scripture is simple and clean. He married her, he impregnated her, she bore a son. No ceremony is mentioned. The study authors have failed to notice that God does not palaver or talk trivia when He states His case. There is no folderol in the Book of Ruth.

Over the centuries, man's interpretations of the Bible have prevailed, have been repeated and accepted, again and again. We are not inclined to question the gospel "according to man." All of which brings us to the Book of Ruth, the strong contradiction to man's wisdom and the testament to God's equally strong celebration of same-sex relationships.

I have watched numerous videos about the Book of Ruth, and they all have some variation of Boaz's seduction of Ruth, and the elaborate pomp and circumstance of marriage. One video boldly states that Ruth asked Boaz to marry her. Those words and word pictures do not appear in Scripture. Instead, Scripture speaks clearly and simply of Ruth's acknowledgement of her place in Boaz's life. She understands that he is the lawful redeemer, not a suitor. Each speaks of Boaz's legal responsibilities.

Now, let's talk about the redemption of these women, and how Ruth and Naomi became the keepers of the lineage of King David and of Jesus Christ, the King of kings.

In the Beginning

Ruth Chapter 1

Inasmuch as God owns these scriptures, He also owns the very transactional nature of the Book of Ruth. In Chapter 1, He lays out the spare groundwork for the narrative of the women in their early days. He also makes clear the purposeful-but-transient nature of the men—husband, sons, and kinsmen.

The plot is set. In five verses and 142 words (AMP) God dismisses the normal lay of the land in which men dominate by the laws of the time and plainly puts the women's futures in their own hands—and in His.

After the years in Moab, Naomi learns that the LORD is feeding the people of Judah, her people, and decides to return home. Naomi's state of mind is important. The premise of the Bible studies of Ruth is that Naomi learns that the famine is over and responds to that information to return to Bethlehem.

The commentaries also foster the idea that Naomi is bereft of feelings for her LORD. However, in His scripture Naomi responds to word that the LORD is back to aid His people, not that the famine is over. This becomes a significant point later in this chapter. Nothing in Scripture suggests that Naomi feels that the LORD has indeed forsaken her. In fact, she is hopeful, which is why she is making the trip.

The news of the LORD being in Bethlehem heartens Naomi, and she and the girls begin their journey to that city (Ruth 1:6).

Although it is unclear how far Naomi and the girls had traveled from Moab, Naomi realizes that her daughters, as she now calls them, will face substantial difficulties in Bethlehem. The girls are Moabites, a people who worship idols, a fact that would make the girls unwelcome in Bethlehem.

One Bible study[52] creates the image of an unhappy Naomi who, for whatever reason, does not want to be bothered by these young women any longer. The study author creates a contentious scene in which she suggests that Naomi angrily tries to dismiss the girls. Not a word in this Scripture speaks to any emotionality. Naomi is talking to her girls in earnest about the trials ahead.

Speaking as a woman of Naomi's age who has gone through situations like those Naomi has experienced, I believe that God's words for her speak from a compassionate woman/mother's point of view. Naomi, as the mother and the leader of the family, was imploring these young women to think about the cold, hard facts of their situation. For instance. she knew that they would need to have husbands in Bethlehem, and she clearly was no longer able to help them with that necessity. The women also were young Moabites, which would present a formidable hurdle for them. Naomi knew that the young Moabite girls would threaten the balance of the male/female relationships in the community. Naomi was not angry; she was being protective of her girls.

In 1:8-9: Naomi said to her two daughters-in-law, "Go back, each of you return to your mother's house. May the LORD show kindness to you as you have shown kindness to the dead and to me. May the LORD grant that you find rest, each one in the home of her husband." Please note that God has written that Naomi urged her daughters-in-law to "return to your mother's house," not "your father's house." This is, I believe, further affirmation of woman's importance to God's message in this book of the Bible and to history.

In these verses, Naomi shares the wisdom and the knowledge of her years with the young women, Orpah and Ruth. Contrary to the studies, Naomi is not impatient with them. Again, speaking as a woman of Naomi's age and circumstances, I believe that she feels the uneasiness and the responsibility for her daughters-in-law. Based upon the marrying practices of those times, the girls probably were young and had never been anywhere other than Moab. Moreover, the three of them had lived in close company for a decade or so, and their familiar family unit was what the girls knew and depended upon. As their mother, Naomi considered the struggles facing them.

First, Naomi knew the arduous trip, 50 miles (the distance from Moab to Bethlehem) on foot, would be daunting. She had completed that trip once and knew what might well lie ahead. Second, the women of Bethlehem would be unlikely to welcome idolaters, especially young women seeking husbands from among their men. So, I believe, Naomi did what any conscientious mother would do: try her best to persuade the girls to stay with their families and safety in Moab.

Naomi kissed them goodbye, and they wept. Breaking up the family unit was painful. They didn't want to leave Naomi. (1:10) And they said to her, "No, we will go with you to your people [in Judah]." The young women must have felt some fear about the trip home alone, along with the pain of losing the stability of Naomi's love and support.

Nevertheless, Naomi knew that her returning to Bethlehem without the protection of a man was going to be difficult enough, without adding the girls to her dilemma. Women were nothing without a man in those days. Widows lived as paupers. In 1:13, Naomi says ". . . No, my daughters; for it is much more difficult for me than for you because the LORD'S hand has gone against me." The mother is saying that she was too old and of limited options. Furthermore, she would have to rely upon the kindly fulfillment of the laws of Judah that protect widows. Without Elimelech or her sons, Naomi herself was vulnerable. Again, she urged the girls to choose safety in Moab, not in her company, which would be fraught with challenges.

Upon Naomi's second petition (1:13), Orpah relented and turned toward Moab. Ruth on the other hand, was not having it. Naomi tried once more, useless though her effort was, to persuade Ruth to join Orpah. It is here that God's words show and emphasize that He would not deter or deny Ruth's love for Naomi. He certainly could have written the Scripture quite differently if that had been His intention. More to the point, He could have omitted this heartfelt declaration of love. Instead, this powerful passage defines the foundation of the Book of Ruth and its ultimate purpose: the anointing and the celebration of same-sex relationships.

Some commentaries refer to this passage as Ruth's "loyalty pledge" to Naomi. Please. A loyalty pledge is what the Girl Scouts recite at meetings. The Pledge of Allegiance to the Flag of the United States of America is a loyalty pledge. What God wrote for Ruth are words of an impassioned, loving commitment. Were that not true, I doubt that millions upon millions of couples through the millennia would have affirmed or reaffirmed their love, one for the other, with a banal loyalty pledge.

In 1:14, God writes "Then they wept aloud again; and Orpah kissed her mother-in-law [goodbye], but Ruth clung to her."

Again, Naomi appealed to Ruth's good sense (1:15-17). "Look, your sister-in-law has gone back to her people and to her gods; turn back and follow your sister." Still, Ruth clung to Naomi, and God gave Ruth this profound, ageless soliloquy to speak to Naomi (1:16-17) "Do not urge me to leave you or to turn back from following you; for where you go, I will go, and where you lodge, I will lodge. Your people will be my people, and your God, my God. Where you die, I will die, and there I will be buried. May the LORD do the same to me [as He has done to you], and more also, if anything but death separates me from you." Please note, Ruth spoke of "the LORD," not "your LORD." I believe that God's choice of words tells us that Ruth has become one of His.

I repeat, if you sit with me today and professes your belief in God and in the Bible, then I think that you must also consider, if not believe, that God, not man, wrote these loving words for Ruth. Man, as the self-appointed and sole arbiter of Scripture, does not recognize women, much less acknowledge the Book of Ruth as God's firm hand in this relationship and its importance to His plan, to the future of mankind.

It is important, also, to note that Naomi did not reject Ruth's declaration. She accepted it and moved on. From this point on, God's words show two determined, clever, strong, smart women who are devoted to each other and to their joint life. God wrote no words of trepidation, no words of hesitation, no rebuke, no words questioning what might lie ahead for them. He wrote only words that bespeak their confidence and their trust in themselves and in each other.

The Rev. Jeff Miner,[53] senior pastor at LifeJourney Church, says that in this part of the Scripture, God celebrates their same-sex relationship. Miner says that the word "clung" is significant in God's writing here. "The same Hebrew word (dabaq) that is used in Genesis 2:24 to describe how Adam felt about Eve (and how spouses are supposed to feel toward each other) is used in Ruth 1:14 to describe how Ruth felt about Naomi. Her feelings are celebrated, not condemned."

From my perspective, the words in this Scripture speak of agape love between the women. Agape is Christian love, Christ-like love, which is distinctly different from erotic love or emotional affection. It is, nonetheless, an abiding love.

Moreover, Miner adds that, "Throughout Christian history, Ruth's vow to Naomi has been used to illustrate the nature of the marriage covenant. These words are often read at Christian wedding ceremonies and used in sermons to illustrate the ideal love that spouses should have for one another. The fact that these words were originally spoken by one woman to another tells us a lot about how God feels about same-gender relationships."[54] No matter how the truth of God's words may contradict one's personal opinions, God's words are God's words. They are unrelenting in their strength and intent.

Now, we come to what I believe is a serious misstatement and misrepresentation among the studies: Naomi and her bitterness. When Naomi and Ruth arrived in Bethlehem, the city was "stirred." The women flocked to Naomi and asked, "Is this Naomi?" Remember, at least 10 years had passed since Naomi had felt the closeness of her friends and acquaintances. The women were surprised, yet glad, to see her.

She said to them (1:20-21) "Do not call me Naomi (sweetness); call me Mara (bitter), for the Almighty has caused me great grief and bitterness. I left full [with a husband and two sons], but the LORD has brought me back empty. Why call me Naomi, since the LORD has testified against me, and the Almighty has afflicted me?"

The Bible studies say that Naomi declared that she was bitter and spoke as such. I contend that she never said, "I am bitter." Nowhere in the scripture did Naomi say, imply, or behave as though she was bitter. What she did say is, that the LORD had caused her grief and bitterness. This is true. The deaths of her husband and her sons, without bringing her grandchildren, which a mother anticipates, were painful. "Call me bitter" is not the same as Naomi saying, "I am bitter."

Again, I speak as a woman who has experienced circumstances such as those Naomi had endured. She had been away from her homeland for so long and without the support of these women, beloved women, she had known well in her days in Bethlehem. She was without their comfort to buoy her through the adversity of her relocation and her several bereavements. I see her words "call me bitter" as a heartfelt supplication. What I read in Naomi's words is, "Oh, my sisters, comfort me. I have been away from you for so long, and I have lost so much. My husband and my sons. My heart hurts so. Hug on me. Let me feel your love." The presence and comfort of her friends relieved Naomi's human needs for consolation.

The scripture also does not say that she and her friends cried, but I have to believe tears were shed all around as they comforted her. This was a precious moment. I further believe that Naomi was not bitter or bereft, owing to her reason for returning to Bethlehem. She returned to her homeland expressly because her LORD was there, taking care of His people (and hers). It was this information that drew her back to Bethlehem.

It is important to note that Naomi's return to Bethlehem was beautifully timed. "So, Naomi returned from the country of Moab, and with her Ruth the Moabitess, her daughter-in-law. And they arrived in Bethlehem at the beginning of the barley harvest." (1:22) Man, not God, tangles his thinking with what he believes are coincidences. The many bibles do say that Ruth "happened upon" Boaz's field, which implies that she was there by accident. Seriously? I believe that this is a mistranslation, maybe even a lack of interest in the truth. God makes happen what does happen. Because man neither sees nor accepts the truth of God's broader plan, he sees the women's arrival in Bethlehem at harvest time as a convenient coincidence. However, Ruth and Naomi were right where they needed to be, where God had placed them to further His plan.

The events that occur during the harvest in Chapter 2 of Ruth furthers His narrative.

Gleaning in Boaz's Field
Ruth Chapter 2

Before we begin to look at Chapter 2, let's look at Ruth herself. The various narratives portray her as an unchanging being whom others judge by her country of origin. You know, once a Moabite, always a Moabite. These writers overlook the fact that this is God's story, and His narrative does not judge Ruth. God sees her more clearly because He sees two very important details. One, Ruth, the idolater of false gods, has spent at least a decade in Naomi's godly example. Ruth's life has been shaped by His gift of grace, prevenient grace, through Naomi's abiding love for Him. Two, God sees all pieces of the Book of Ruth and how they affect the outcome that He has planned. He chose Ruth to help Him fulfill this moment.

Prevenient grace, God's gift of persistent and consistent grace when He is calling you to become one of His own, is a strong factor in this portion of the narrative. When God wants you to walk with Him, He lays out many moments in which you can discern the benefit of His presence in your life. Because Ruth is an exceptional part of God's plan for the future of mankind, He began with His gift of Naomi, who was key to Ruth's growing away from idolatry. Naomi was a model of godliness. Ruth's gleaning in Boaz's barley fields is another gift of prevenient grace.

In this chapter of Ruth, God's plan for Naomi and Ruth's redemption, in accordance with the laws of Judea, comes together.

Naomi has returned to her homeland of Bethlehem and knows that she must find the kinsman who would redeem her. In those ancient times, a woman was nothing without a man. However, as Elimelech's widow, Naomi knows that she has two things going for her: Elimelech had owned property that can now be used for her redemption, and Elimelech had kinsmen who can buy that property and redeem her. Redemption in this case means "to restore the deceased to his inheritance." (3:5) Naomi knows the relative is Boaz, but she does not yet know where Boaz lives. She has shared none of this information with Ruth.

In the meantime, Ruth undertakes the business of providing for Naomi and herself through gleaning, a right granted to widows and the poor, and a process that is unfamiliar to her. So, she asks, "Please let me go to the field and glean among the ears of grain after one [of the reapers] in whose sight I might find favor." Naomi agrees. (2:3)

At this point, Ruth, a stranger, seeks the favor of protection in this new land and the unfamiliar endeavor, not the romantic encounter that studies and commentaries insist is the case. (A cursory online search will show how common is the stage version Ruth.) She has pledged her love to Naomi, another moment of grace that Ruth acknowledged. Ruth remains unaware that the field in which she gleans is the connection between Boaz and their redemption. Nonetheless, she gleans diligently throughout the day for their joint wellbeing.

When Boaz returned from Bethlehem, he noticed the new person in his field. He asked his servant for information, and his servant gave a positive, perfunctory account of Ruth's time in the field. Boaz was not at all bothered by the fact that Ruth was Moabite. Except for the casual reference to her homeland in the servant's report, Scripture does not emphasize Ruth's nationality. When he spoke with her, Boaz said he had heard the news of Naomi and Ruth in the city and recounted Ruth's sacrifices on Naomi's behalf.

"I have been made fully aware of everything that you have done for your mother-in-law since the death of your husband, and how you have left your mother and father and the land of your birth and have come to a people that you did not know before. May the LORD repay you for your kindness, and may your reward be full from the LORD, the God of Israel, under whose wings you have come to take refuge." (2: 11,12) Notice, Boaz made no reference to Ruth being a Moabitess. He speaks of her only as a stranger.

Boaz behaved with the demeanor of the well-bred wealthy landowner that he was. He also behaved with the gentility and the confidence that speaks of knowing the rightness of walking with God. Ruth responded to his kindness and took care to let him know that she understood that she was an outsider in this land. Ruth still does not know that she is in the right place at the right time.

Then she said, "Let me find favor in your sight, my lord, for you have comforted me and have spoken kindly to your maidservant, though I am not as one of your maidservants." (2:13) Ruth did not yet know that she was sitting with the sought-after kinsman, their redeemer.

This thoughtful, honest exchange is one of landowner to a maidservant who is deserving of special treatment because of her diligence as a worker and because he knows of her association with Naomi, not because of any sexual desires, as some narratives insist, with a knowing waggle of the eyebrows. Ruth is, at this point, a woman of interest to Boaz only as the woman who is associated with Naomi, his kinsman's widow. At mealtime, Boaz invited Ruth to eat some bread dipped in vinegar. He did not, however, invite Ruth to his table, neither did she assume that advantage. She ate at the reaper's table. Boaz granted Ruth still more favors before she returned to Naomi.

When she prepared to return to her gleaning, Boaz ordered his servants, "Let her glean even among the sheaves, and do not insult her. Also, you shall purposely pull out for her some stalks [of grain] from the sheaves and leave them so that she may collect them, and do not rebuke her." (2:15, 16) Boaz was behaving in keeping with their respective social stations. Contrary to the various Bible studies, Boaz was not trying to seduce Ruth. God's words for Boaz do not even hint at any romantic alliance.

Boaz's respect for Ruth, with no reference to her heritage, is yet another example of God's prevenient grace.

I believe it is important to note here that Ruth was far from the frightened, frail girl as commentaries are inclined to portray her. Ruth gleaned from morning to evening. Then, she beat the grain from the florets and gathered the grain together. Scripture says that she beat about a bushel, which she carried to the city. However, Scripture does not say how far she carried her bushel of barley, or that she had to be one sturdy, determined woman. A bushel of barley weighs about 48 pounds. In comparison, two plastic-wrapped cases of 24 bottles of water weigh about 52 pounds.

When Ruth returned home, Naomi tied the loose ends together. Ruth related her experience in gleaning, her encounter with Boaz, and the many favors he had bestowed upon her, including his admonition wrapped in a generous invitation. Ruth should, "Stay close to my servants until they have harvested my entire crop." (2:21) It is reasonable to conclude that Boaz was protecting Ruth from the probable sexual advances from his workers. Men will be men, especially when they are eager to know new flesh, as they so brutally demonstrated in Sodom and Gomorrah.

At this point, Naomi began sharing her knowledge of Boaz and of his importance to them. She also acknowledged and understood Boaz's protection and generosity.

Naomi said to Ruth, "It is good, my daughter, for you to go out [to work] with his maids, so that others do not assault you in another field." So, she stayed close to Boaz's maids, gleaning until the end of the barley and wheat harvests. And she lived with her mother-in-law. (2: 22, 23)

I believe God added the fact that Ruth continued to live

with Naomi to focus attention on the certainty that Ruth was with Naomi and had exhibited no love interest in Boaz.

Ruth's story has arrived at Boaz's critical negotiation for the lawful redemption of the women, and the men's final appearance in the Book of Ruth.

Redemption is Guaranteed
Ruth Chapter 3

We are at the point of the women's redemption. Naomi knows Boaz is near at hand, and she lays out her plan to gain their redemption. As a former resident of Bethlehem, Naomi is familiar with the practices associated with gleaning. She also knows how to achieve redemption, the lawful action of making widows, such Ruth and she, whole before the law. Women without men were nothing, except bothersome paupers.

God's influence is ever-present in this chapter of Ruth.

In verses two through four (Ruth 3: 2-4), Naomi instructs Ruth in how to prepare herself to meet Boaz that night and how to begin the contact that would facilitate their goal of gaining redemption. Without question or hesitation, Ruth perfumed herself and dressed in clothing that enhanced her individuality, rather than garments that would remind Boaz of Ruth the gleaner.

Ruth went to the threshing floor, concealing herself and watching, as Naomi had directed, until Boaz had fallen asleep. Then, Ruth went to lie at Boaz's feet, also as Naomi had instructed. Ruth pulled the cover from Boaz's feet over her. Lying at the feet of a man in those circumstances was the custom of the ladies of the night, but not that of Ruth. She was there on the business of their future, not monkey business. Naomi had told Ruth that Boaz would know the purpose of Ruth's presence, and that he would complete his part of the covenant. Naomi trusted herself, her experience, and her God.

During the night, Boaz awakened. Probably because Ruth had taken his foot cover, or maybe he had felt her heat against his feet. The point is, Boaz was not expecting anyone to share his covers. Although the various narratives imply that a sexual assignation was intended, Scripture says otherwise.

"Who are you?" Boaz asks of the person at his feet in the dark. (3:9) Ruth does not hesitate. "I am Ruth your maid. Spread the hem of your garment over me, for you are a close relative and redeemer." Ruth knows what she's about and clearly stated her intent; she was seeking her redeemer, not a lover. In the practice of the time, the man spreads his garment over the woman as the signal that sex was possible. Some studies have Ruth blatantly asking Boaz to marry her, which is a lot of hooey. Boaz knew what covering Ruth with his garment meant, but his intent was as clear as Ruth's. He praised Ruth for her judicious behavior and added "May you be blessed by the LORD, my daughter. You have made your last kindness better than the first; for you have not gone after young men, whether poor or rich." (3:10)

Boaz was well aware of his place in her life, and that place was not as a random lover. Thus, he began to fulfill the law of Judea. Boaz not only showed humble respect for Ruth, but he also acknowledged her reputation. ". . . All of my people in the city know that you are a woman of excellence." (3:11) Again, he uttered not a single word about her being a Moabite. It also seems clear that Boaz knew that Ruth represented Naomi.

Boaz told Ruth to finish the night there, but she left before sunlight. Boaz promised Ruth that, although she had a closer relative than he, if that relative did not redeem her, then he would. (3:13) Boaz then instructed his people to say nothing about Ruth being on the threshing floor that night and sent Ruth home with six measures of barley, so that she would not return to Naomi empty-handed. Boaz respected Ruth and protected her reputation.

When Ruth reported the events of the night to Naomi, Naomi knew that the die had been cast. What was supposed to happen would happen. Naomi's trust was great.

Then Naomi said to Ruth, "Sit and wait, my daughter, until you learn how this matter turns out; for the man will not rest until he has settled it today." (3:18)

In the 523 carefully chosen words in this chapter of Ruth, God wrote no side trips into what Boaz might be thinking about the night before, or a possible future with Ruth. Instead, God wrote the strong bones of Boaz's awareness of duty and his promise to Ruth. No love affair was developing, despite what the variety of narratives and Bible studies would have us believe.

In verses 10 and 11, the transactional nature of the encounter was indisputable. Ruth identified herself and his place in her life. Boaz respectfully acknowledged his role as Ruth's redeemer and vowed to fulfill it. No matter what. He acknowledged that a relative more qualified than he should be given the first opportunity to fulfill the law. If, however, that man failed to meet his responsibility, then he, Boaz, would assure that redemption.

All that remains is for Boaz to strike the deal with the closer relative that would return Naomi and Ruth to full rights as residents of Bethlehem.

The Deal is Struck

Ruth Chapter 4

God wrote a concise version of what He wanted to accomplish. He established that the women—Naomi and Ruth—were the ones who would rock the cradle of the lineage of kings. Boaz has some bargaining yet to do. Then, when the agreement is completed, God dismisses Boaz from the final scenes in this story. He relegates Boaz to the honor roll of Begat Boys. You know. The lengthy list of men in Genesis who planted their seed in the fertile women who would produce life after life after life. The Begat Boys for Ruth's lineage appear in verse 17 of last chapter in Ruth. The balance of the story of Ruth rests in the hands of this capable same-sex couple and the women of Bethlehem.

The next morning, as Ruth told Naomi of the events of the night on the threshing floor, Boaz set out for Bethlehem to settle the matter of Naomi and Ruth's redemptions as heirs of Elimelech and Mahlon, respectively. First, he called Elimelech's closest relative over to sit with him at the city's gate, where business and legal matters were completed. Then Boaz gathered 10 elders of the city, men, of course, to witness the transaction. With no holds barred or information withheld, God writes:

He said to the closest relative (name not recorded), "Naomi, who has returned from the country of Moab, must sell the plot of land which belonged to our brother, Elimelech. I thought to let you hear of it, saying, buy it in the presence of those sitting here, and before the elders of my people. If you will redeem it, redeem it; but if not, then tell me, so that I may know; for there is no one besides you to redeem it, and I am [next of kin] after you." (4:3,4)

Mr. Anonymous agreed to redeem it. He agreed, that is, until Boaz added that Ruth the Moabitess, the widow of the Mahlon, came with the property. She must be redeemed, too, in order "to restore the name of the deceased to his inheritance." Mr. Anonymous said, "I cannot redeem it for myself, because [by marrying a Moabitess] I would jeopardize my own inheritance. Take my right of redemption yourself because I cannot redeem it." (4:6) The deal was sealed when Mr. Anonymous pulled off his sandal, gave it to Boaz, as was the custom of the day, and limped off down the dusty city street. With that, Boaz announced to the crowd that they had witnessed his purchase ". . . (of) everything that was Elimelech's and every-thing that was Mahlon's and Chilion's from the hand of Naomi. I also have acquired Ruth the Moabitess, the widow of Mahlon, to be my wife to restore the name of the deceased to his inheritance . . ." (4: 9-10)

Now, God knew that Mr. Anonymous would never be the redeemer because Boaz was His man for the job. He had planned it that way. God's plan received resounding praise for the cove-nant between Mr. Anonymous and Boaz. The elders and all the people at the gate declared, "We are witnesses. May the LORD make the woman who is coming into your house like Rachael and Leah, the two who built the household of Israel." (4:11) The witnesses were cheerleaders for God's plan. Notice, too, that God reiterates the roles of Rachael and Leah, who established the household of Israel.

In the praise from those assembled, God established His plan to designate Naomi and Ruth to build the lineage of kings, just as Rachael and Leah had built the household of Israel.

The events in verse 13 end the part of any male in this story. "So, Boaz took Ruth, and she became his wife. And he went in to her, and the LORD enabled her to conceive, and she gave birth to a son." That Ruth gave birth to a boy was part of God's preordained plan. Boaz came, made his eight-second deposit in his woman, the bank of humanity. In a couple of sentences, Boaz was gone. The Scripture recorded no wedding nonsense for Boaz and Ruth or birth announcement or distribution of cigars among Boaz's many friends, or whatever men did to celebrate a birth in ancient days. Boaz married Ruth and disappeared into history.

However, the women of Bethlehem were in tune with God's plan to celebrate this same-sex couple.

Then the women said to Naomi, "Blessed be the LORD who has not left you without a redeemer [grandson, as heir] today, and may his name become famous in Israel. May he also be to you one who restores life and sustains your old age; for your daughter-in-law, who loves you and is better to you than seven sons, has given birth to him." (4:14,15) The women had accepted Ruth and Naomi as a couple.

God then celebrated the women with a modest miracle (which may be an oxymoron). He made Naomi the child's nurse (4:16). Because Ruth was not mentioned again in connection with her baby, I concluded that He had granted Naomi the supply of milk that would sustain the child. If He could make possible the birth of a son to Sarah, 90, and Abraham, 99, He sure as the dickens could make it possible for Naomi to suckle Ruth's babe.

Another point in verse 17 accentuates the fact that Boaz is out of the picture. The assembled women named the baby, saying, "A son [grandson] has been born to Naomi." They named him Obed [worshipper]. He is the father of Jesse, [who is] the father of David [the ancestor of Jesus Christ]. (4:17) This is important because, in the tradition of the times, the man named the child. The mother might suggest a name, but the father had the final authority. God granted the women in Ruth's and Naomi's circle of friends the honor of naming the ancestor of David.

God made very clear in the Book of Ruth that He had blessed all who would proceed from that day to the birth of His son, Jesus

Christ. He foretold this in the Book of Ruth, included in the Old Testament, many centuries before Christ was born.

We add a note of irony here. In keeping with the popular history, the lineage of kings began in Bethlehem through God's anointing and celebrating Naomi and Ruths same-sex relationship and the birth of Obed. Insofar as we know, the lineage ended in Bethlehem with the birth of Jesus Christ, through His anointing of the Virgin Mary. Women, not men, were called to these special roles in securing the future of mankind.

From these many blessings came Christianity.

God anointed this relationship, but man has spent centuries maligning same-sex relationships to prove that God created something so displeasing that it immediately was a sin of its own. When men or women, write about or teach about Ruth, they usually speak of the story in the traditional way: Frail woman in strange land needs a benefactor, and she engages the acceptable seduction to accomplish her ends. Not only is Ruth not a fanciful love story, but it also is foundational to God's plan of acceptance for same-sex relationships.

Not a wise move to challenge God's wisdom. Yet, man remains confident in his ill-advised impertinence.

Now, it's time to tell David's story.

What About David and Jonathan?

God has given us two examples of how He has anointed and celebrated same-sex relationships, and those examples have been with us since the first Bible was published. We began with the story of Ruth and Naomi, in which He celebrated their relationship by entrusting the lineage of kings to them. The second story is that of David and Jonathan, two young warriors. God was so mellow with their relationship that he eventually proclaimed David as King of Israel. David also was Ruth's great grandson.

God granted great favor to these two couples—Ruth and Naomi and David and Jonathan. Hmm. I believe we can call these relationships evidence of the purposefulness and the rightness of God's plan to integrate same-sex relationships into our lives. According to my reading, it appears that David and Jonathan were bisexual. Both men had wives, and other women. Yet, these facts did not dampen their ardor for each another.

Man, the trusted spokesman for God in the pulpit, has for centuries disregarded the lesson of Ruth, probably because the story was about two presumed needy women, saved by a man through the law of redemption. Women need men, you know. Yet, in Ruth we saw how quickly God dispatched the men from the story. Women were property in those days, and man didn't need them. As evidenced by man's recent overturning of laws that affect women's very existence, women continue to be property.

Contrary to the Book of Ruth, the lesson of David and Jonathan in 1 Samuel was about strapping young men behaving outside of King Saul's expectations and the expectations of current-day man. What is there to say about a couple of guys who were best buddies? Oh, yeah, David slew Goliath, and he was a revered warrior. We know all of that. David also was a bit of a scoundrel, a man who knew many women and owned several of them as wives.

In retrospect, I recall how a couple of friends and I have engaged in some tense discussions about David and his questionable escapades. I saw David the Scoundrel as God's pet. Yet another spoiled male, as it were. He had impregnated Bathsheba. Then, he had her husband killed in battle, so the husband didn't learn that David not only coveted his wife but also had impregnated her. Along with his other capers, it seemed to me that David's reckless behavior should have warranted some punishment. My friend argued that I should remember that God had a plan for David. She was correct. Instead of punishment, God made him King of Israel.

However, what is true for David is that he demonstrated his full faith and trust in the LORD. Our faith in Him, even the faith of His favorite ne'er-do-well, defines the seminal difference to Him. Faith and trust are all He wants from any of us. So long as we repent of our sinful behavior, everything we do, no matter how objectionable it is to any of us, He forgives us and moves on. "He has removed our sins as far from us as the east is from the west. The Lord is like a father to his children, tender and compassionate to those who fear him. For he knows how weak we are." (Psalm 103:12-14)

Still, the God Wannabes hold to their misconceptions. They remain unable to see or to accept that the inextricable bond between David and Jonathan was soul to soul, and that God's word declared it as such. They were one, those young men. Not so, man has declared. They were just good friends, fist bumps, solid comrades. Nothing more than the male-bonding rituals. The other scenario, the real-life experience, is unacceptable to those who presume to be wiser than God or have no concept of what God-blessed love is about.

Nevertheless, the words about the relationship between David and Jonathan in 1 and 2 Samuel are specific. This story is about two young men who love each other, soul mates. But deduce for yourself. Let the words of Scripture, not the flawed, self-serving interpretation of Scripture from the God Wannabes, show you the way.

This story begins with young David returning home, having slain that pesky giant, Goliath, with his slingshot and some stones. He is talking with King Saul. Our scene opens with Saul, David, and Jonathan in 1 Samuel 1:1-4

"When David had finished speaking to Saul, the soul of Jonathan was bound to the soul of David, and Jonathan loved him as his own soul. Saul took him that day and would not let him return to his father's house. Then Jonathan made a covenant with David, because he loved him as his own soul. Jonathan stripped himself of the robe he was wearing, and gave it to David, and his armor, and even his sword and his bow and his belt."

This scene is not your typical chest bump between two guys who just got home from summer camp. In my day, we would have said that Jonathan swooned at David's feet, so overcome was he with the emotion in the heat, or, maybe, the soul of the moment. Jonathan's words and actions were those of one person, impassioned by the stunning soul connection to another who received them in full measure. Such nonsense, you say. If that is your reaction, then I suspect that you have never shared such a profound connection. I am genuinely sad for you.

David grew as a warrior and in popularity in Israel. Saul feared David. Actually, David twisted Saul's mind in several ways. For one, David's prowess as a warrior was unparalleled primarily because, as Saul knew, that God was with David. For another, Saul had been grooming Jonathan to take over as king when Saul's days were done. Now, Prince Jonathan was, Saul believed, David's plaything, which made Jonathan subservient in King Saul's mind. Surely Jonathan was allowing himself to be the subordinate one. (There's that penetration thing again.), This behavior is unbefitting a man who was in line to be king. This angered Saul, but his anger gave weight to the truth of the bonding of souls between David and Jonathan.

One day, Saul, also a warrior of some repute, was turning a javelin in his hand, as he argued with Jonathan. "And Saul cast the javelin; for he said, I will smite David even to the wall with it. And David avoided out of his presence twice." (1 Samuel 18:11) Jonathan bolted from his father's presence. Saul was one angry king. The thought of David's companionship threatened Saul, and Saul began contriving ways to kill David.

Well, Saul's convoluted plans did not work out. David continued to prevail, as did David and Jonathan's relationship.

Not to belabor the agitation in Saul's house, but tension was great. The pot boiled over one night when Saul's fear of David and his anger over of Jonathan's love for David took hold. During one of these "Father-knows-best" battles at the table, Jonathan ran away and sought David to tell him that they had to stop seeing each other. They had to go their separate ways because the tension with Saul was too dangerous. Saul, unlike the God Wannabes, was fully aware of the depth of the young men's relationship. The male-male sex was not the issue, however. Saul objected to it because in that relationship, his son was no better than a submissive woman, not the behavior of a king. The relationship angered Saul.

". . . David rose from beside the stone heap and prostrated himself with his face to the ground. He bowed three times, and they kissed each other and wept with each other; David wept the more. Then Jonathan said to David, 'Go in peace, since both of us have sworn in the name of the Lord, saying, The Lord shall be between me and you, and between my descendants and your descendants, forever'" He got up and left; and Jonathan went into the city. (1 Samuel 20: 41-42)

The notice of their covenant was simple. "Then Jonathan and David made a covenant, because he loved him as his own soul." (1 Samuel 18:3) However, the covenant itself is as impassioned as their relationship. Jonathan speaks, "But show me unfailing kindness like the Lord's kindness as long as I live, so that I may not be killed, and do not ever cut off your kindness from my family— not even when the Lord has cut off every one of David's enemies from the face of the earth." So, Jonathan made a covenant with the house of David, saying, "May the Lord call David's enemies to account." Out of his love for David, Jonathan had him reaffirm his oath, because Jonathan loved David as he loved himself. (1 Samuel 20:14-17) The words of this Scripture reaffirm the bond between the young men. No interpretation is necessary.

The word "covenant," spoken between the men, has allowed the God Wannabes to call David and Jonathan's relationship nothing more than a strong friendship. Bilge water! The agreement between the men was on a separate matter. Their relationship remained genuine, not merely a contract to be honored.

In moments like these, I find it confounding that people who say they believe and trust in God have such trouble accepting the concept that God created the genetics that allow same-sex relationships. They would rather believe that homosexuals are fraught with the plague from evil pixie dust blown from some secret garden, than that they are God's children.

Continuing with the story of David and Jonathan, the Rev. Jeff Miner writes, "Under inspiration of the Holy Spirit, the author of 1 and 2 Samuel wrote this beautiful love story and saw no conflict between it and the earlier Scriptures in Leviticus. How is this possible? Apparently, the author of 1 and 2 Samuel understood the Leviticus passage the same way we do, seeing it as a condemnation of Canaanite temple sex, which, therefore, had no application to a deep romantic relationship between two men who loved and served the God of Israel."

Well, Saul and Jonathan went off to war. Word came from

the battlefield that Saul and Jonathan were dead. The messenger returned to David. When he arrived, the messenger fell to the ground to honor David and gave Saul's crown and armband to him.

"Then David and all the men with him took hold of their clothes and tore them. They mourned and wept and fasted till evening for Saul and his son Jonathan, and for the army of the Lord and for the nation of Israel, because they had fallen by the sword." (2 Samuel 1:11-12)

David's show of grief did not end there. David also tore his clothes and fasted. He wept and wrote a song. Furthermore, David ordered all of Judah to sing it. The song contained words of pain for Jonathan and words that publicly affirmed David's love for him.

> "Saul and Jonathan, beloved and lovely!
> in life and in death they were not divided;
> they were swifter than eagles,
> they were stronger than lions.
> How the mighty have fallen in the midst of battle!
> Jonathan lies slain upon your high places.
> I am distressed for you my brother, Jonathan;
> Greatly beloved were you to me;
> your love to me was wonderful, passing the love of women."
> (2 Samuel 1:23, 26-27)

With God's help, David, God's beloved child, wrote these words of respect, pain, and loss for all to sing and to hear. Just as He wrote the clear, beautiful soliloquy for Ruth, He facilitated David's writing of his pain and loss, and, yes, of his love for Jonathan.

Still, I wonder how can anyone read these words and call the relationship between these two men a sterile relationship or a strong friendship? We are all grownups here. You either believe in God's wisdom, or you do not.

∽

This seems a good time to talk about the difference between a literal interpretation of Scripture and the interpretation founded in fact. The literal interpretation allows the reader to apply current attitudes, mores, and thinking to the ancient biblical text. Interpretation of Scripture founded in fact centers the meaning of the text on the customs, the attitudes, and history of the time in which the Scripture was written. The literal interpretation of Scripture allows the reader to select bit and pieces of Scripture in which the words "support" the reader's premised. Scholars call these "clobber passages" or "proof texts."

The ever-popular literal translation of the rewritten Leviticus is an excellent example. Man latched onto the words "You must not lie with a man as with a woman. That is an abomination" (Leviticus 18:22) as a prohibition of same-sex relationships. Those words from ancient times interpreted in the context of today's belief system, a literal translation, could indeed mean what man wants them to mean. In the truth of the times, the language and mores and customs, those words refer specifically to a code of conduct that focused on the maintaining the purity of the Jews over the Gentiles and the abomination of pederasty that flourished in the temple. That Scripture had nothing to do with what we know as homosexuality. Homosexuality couldn't have been the topic. If you recall, homosexuality is a 19th century word, which makes it an inappropriate addition to the ancient text.

There also exists a difference between what the God Wannabes interpretation of Scripture and what is written. The stories of Ruth and David are good examples. Ruth herself, with the help of God, spoke the heartfelt words to Naomi. No one can deny that Ruth said those words. It is not open to interpretation. David said of Jonathan: "Greatly beloved were you to me; your love to me was wonderful, passing the love of women." He wrote that declaration and demanded that everyone acknowledge his assertion by singing those passionate words: "Your love to me was wonderful, passing the love of women." No interpretation needed.

One can twist the words and their intent to suit one's limited vision of truth, but, as Aldous Huxley wrote, "Facts do not cease to exist because they are ignored."

∽

We have spent considerable time in the Old Testament, talking about how the God Wannabes have misinterpreted God's word to meet their needs. The most important lesson, of course, comes from Genesis where we learn that God created everything and, then, He declared that all of it was very good. All that lives on this sphere that we call Earth is a gift from God. We may not like everything God has done or understand it, but that does not change the fact that God's hand created it, and no interpretation is needed.

Now that we are aware of the misused words of God in the Old Testament, let's visit the New Testament, which is supposed to be our focus for a life of love and joy. The New Covenant, as expressed in the New Testament, became our book of record when Christ died on the cross. The God Wannabees continue to resist embracing the holy sacrifice of God's only Son upon the cross. Basically, man thumbs his nose at God's sacrifice because he is incapable of letting go of the Old Testament rules, which benefit his profit motives. Bigotry and judgment sell.

Helminiak writes, "We have no record of Jesus ever speaking about same-sex acts, in either the Gospels in the Bibles nor in the so-called 'gnostic gospels' discovered at Nag Hammadi in 1945. This is telling . . . it implies that Jesus had nothing distinctive to say about the subject and that homosexuality was not a concern of the early church, which preserved his sayings."[55]

There is evidence, however, that Jesus had encountered and recorded at least one same-sex relationship during his ministry.

Remember the story of the centurion who came to Jesus and asked Him to heal his servant? The memorable words were, "And Jesus said to him, 'I will come and heal him.'" The centurion replied,

91

"Lord, I am not worthy to have you come under my roof. But speak the word only, and my servant will be healed." (Matthew 8:7-8)

The explanation here is that the centurion sought Jesus' help for healing. Scholars say the centurion, when he asked for favor, he used language that said he was seeking help for his male sex partner. He specifically used the word *pais*, which Helminiak says, "(Pais) is a word likely to refer to a slave used for male-male sex, and there is non-biblical evidence that pais sometimes meant male lover." [56]

In that time, male-male sex was common (The word homosexual was never used because it did not exist.) Romans used their slaves for sex. Helminiak,[57] again says, "It also was common for soldiers far from home to have a male sexual companion with them." Nevertheless, there remains a distinct difference between male-male sex and the consensual same-sex relationships bound by love and the human spirit. The former declares man's dominance, which demonstrates his obsession with his manhood, the Devil's Joystick.

What did Jesus think about this? Why didn't he rebuke the centurion? Most likely because this sort of behavior had been present since the beginning of time. What is important in this lesson is: Jesus did not rebuke the man for having a male lover. Instead he rewarded the centurion for his undaunted faith in Him. Before the assembled crowd, Jesus said, "I have not found faith this great anywhere in Israel." (Matthew 8:10)

Rev. Jeff Miner asks us to ". . . consider carefully: Who is Lord—Jesus or cultural prejudice?"[58]

Now, let's wrap up the loose ends and share some final thoughts.

The Rest of the Story

Well, the end is here.

This chapter, a summary, is frank. In truth, it appears that the God Wannabes have created their condemnation of homosexuals out of whole cloth for centuries. I have been unable to learn in what century man began his pursuit of this group of God's children or why it happened, though I suspect it happened when someone coined the magic word: homosexual. In truth, I do not care. Man's relentless pursuit of his deadly and unfounded verbal attacks on homosexuals is a living, despicable part of today. When man first turned his back on God's omnipotence is irrelevant. It happened, and the God Wannabes literally rebuke His authority.

When I say man, about what man am I writing? An unhappy, frustrated lone man who started the crusade against homosexuals in his out-of-the-way church. Or the man who stands in the pulpit in a church representing one of the organized religions? Doesn't matter. There is no excuse for either one. Satan owns both of them through their shameless weakness and hubris in that weakness. Still does. Why? Because man believes he is greater than God in certain matters. God created everything and said, in Genesis, that His creation was very good. However, by his behavior, man is saying, "No, God. You've got it wrong. The homosexuals are not one of 'us.' We reject them and will keep them from participating in our churches. They are unworthy."

Man, in his willing ignorance of the subject, has interpreted

certain scriptures to give credence to his contention that homosexuals are bodies of sin, in and of themselves. The God Wannabes
insist that this group of God's children has inflicted untold violence
upon the world because of that sin. Scholars call these specially
selected passages clobber passages or proof texts. They are, as
you might surmise, Scripture manipulated to "prove" the accuracy
of the God Wannabes' vehement assertions about homosexuals.

Jesus and His Father, however, presented affirmations to the
contrary. Remember Jesus and the centurion in Matthew? Jesus
is so indifferent in the centurion's relationship with his servant
that He publicly praised the man for his exceptional faith in him,
Jesus. The crowd also had heard the centurion's plea to Jesus and
Jesus' affirmation of centurion's faith. Nothing more needed to be
said. Rather than rebuke the centurion, Jesus declared that the
centurion's deep faith alone proved him worthy of God's favor.

Regardless of how man has twisted Scripture to meet his
pernicious goals, God has demonstrated His favor for same-sex
relations in many ways. Let's build a nutshell summary for the
examples of God's anointing of same-sex relationships that I have
included in my text.

• **Genesis:** In two verses, Genesis 1:26-27, God declared He
had created everything, and that everything that He created was
good. The "everything" is a definitive statement. He notes not a
single exception. In later Scripture, Genesis 1:31, God declared
that His creation was very good.

• **The Book of Ruth:** This book of Scripture also is a definitive statement. God put the lineage of kings in the hands of two
capable women who were devoted to their LORD and to each other.
Just as Rachael and Leah had established the house of Israel, God
committed the lineage of kings to the capable hands of Ruth and
Naomi. That lineage extended to His son Jesus Christ, the King of
kings, and prophesied the lineage from that day forward.

The relationship between Naomi and Ruth could well be a

strong example of agape love. No sexual attraction is intimated, but Ruth's devotion to Naomi, according to Scripture, is complete and unswerving.

• **David and Jonathan:** In 1 and 2 Samuel, God firmly established this as a same-sex relationship. The text, clearly and without apology, shows a soul-to-soul relationship of boundless love between these two young men. Scripture is firm in its certitude of their relationship.

Man, in his failure to accept God's word, turned this soulful, truthful relationship into a pointless connection, a relationship assured only by a sterile contract. The words that God placed in Scripture speak loudly of the heart-felt impact on anyone who walks with God. Those who are tangled in the Gordian knot of some hide-bound religious doctrine continue to clutch their pearls, or whatever is within reach, when David and Jonathan's relationship is mentioned.

I think it is possible here that God wants us to know that love is love. No sexual involvement is intimated. Yet man, impelled by his obsession with his penis, the Devil's Joystick, insists that we look away from his bad behavior. It's all about the DJ. God's concept of love exceeds man's erotic, romantic sense of love.

Additionally, a genetic link exists between Ruth and David. She is his great grandmother. This raises the question about another genetic probability: Is homosexuality a genetic trait? In Chapter 3, we explain the scientific view of the topic.

• **Leviticus and Sodom and Gomorrah:** We shall take these aberrations and the assertions of the God Wannabes together. Yes, they had to do with men and sex. Scripture after Scripture calls attention to men and their preoccupation with sex and the male hierarchy. That practice continues.

Leviticus was about maintaining the separation of the Jews and Gentiles. The Jews were "pure," the Gentiles were gross, to the Jewish thinking. Before man changed the text, Leviticus also was about male prostitution in the temples and pederasty, using male children as sex objects. Until 1983, homosexuality was not a factor in the behaviors advanced in Leviticus. Armed with the new word, man dismissed the original text and added homosexual. Don't look at the evil man does (pederasty), in the ancient text. Follow our illusion: the abominable homosexual.

As I followed lead after lead in my research, I was repelled by the overwhelming abuse to mankind that has been driven by the Devil's Joystick. Penis, the appropriate anatomical term for this body part, is such a soft name for the appendage that drives man's abuse of man and woman. Power tool, or DJ, seems much more accurate. In Leviticus, Satan had a firm grasp on man's weakness for his power tool and salaciously led him around by it.

Male prostitution in the temple, pederasty, was the biblical object of scorn in Scripture. If the term pederasty is strange to you, let's put it into perspective. Pederasty, the molestation of boys, is what some Catholic priests and some men in the Boy Scouts, financially supported by nearly every major religious sect, have freely practiced for heaven knows how long. And, now, we learn that the Baptists have joined into the games of pederasty and more.

The same kind of abuse was true in the fall of Sodom and Gomorrah. The men who were raging outside Lot's home were not seeking any homosexual alliances. No, they were heterosexual males driven by the need to rape the men (angels) inside the home, the need to satisfy the urges of their beloved power tool.

God stomped Satan and his followers. He burned the cities to ashes because man had fallen in league with the devil and failed to provide hospitality, among other abominations. He could find not a single righteous person among the inhabitants. The men thought only of themselves, not of God's admonitions to care for the sick, the poor, the hungry, the elderly, among other imperatives. Homosexuality was not a part of God's thinking in Sodom, nor that of Satan who, once again, firmly grasped the emotional weakness of those men.

The rise and the fall of the Devil's Joystick has so driven history that, in ancient times, warriors brought men along to the battlefield for sex. This is one time that I am grateful that the men were so dismissive of women.

• **Homosexuality in the Bible:** To reiterate, until 1946, the word homosexual did not appear in the original bibles. Moreover, until the late 1860s, homosexual was not even a word in our vocabulary. Now, the God Wannabes assert and insist that their inclusion of the word in Scripture in 1983 justifies their condemnation of homosexuals. In fact, man added the word to shore up his contention that God abhors homosexuality. Nevertheless, we need to think about the validity of man's modern addition of this charged word in sacred text, written thousands of years before the word existed. The addition seems rather suspicious and ego-serving. The God Wannabes are so overcome with self-interest, they make a mockery of Scripture.

If the word homosexual was not part of the written or the spoken lexicon, the body of language used thousands of years ago when the Bible was written, by what authority does man include it now? Is this inclusion not a perversion of the integrity of Scripture and God's flawless creation of everything? What other perversions has man surreptitiously slipped into the Bible?

What does this say about the God Wannabes, the men who stand in the pulpit and pretend to serve God? Are they not actively working against God? Remarkably, they preach in His name, but their words are not reflective of the commandment, "Love thy neighbor as you love yourself." Are their assertions not a sin against God and the Third Commandment, committed while they point their righteous fingers at homosexuals?

By not taking seriously the verses in Genesis as God's truth, man systematically turned the natural evolution of God's plan into something shameful. The God Wannabes have become snakes squirming in the basket of the most devious snake charmer of all,

Satan. Slowly, methodically, he weaves back and forth, enticing them in their incessant need to be important, and they believe and weave. Satan has not only helped them perpetrate the lie about homosexuals, but he also has enjoined the devotion of a legion of women who believe the words of their men, no matter what.

One cannot both serve God and work against Him by bullying His children. God has said that we cannot serve two masters. Does man not take this to heart?

Man's delusion of power has been deadly, demeaning, disgraceful, and embarrassing to millions of God's children for centuries.

∾

A Word to the Parents of Homosexuals:

I have met you. I know your anguish for your child, but I must ask: Why do you grieve so? Do you not believe the words in Genesis? That God created everything and declared that His creations were good, very good? If you believe in God and in Scripture, as you say you do, Mother, then how is it possible for you not understand that the compact package that grew in your womb would become the full-grown adult that He planned? This "terrible thing" that torments you is not a "thing" at all. It did not befall your innocent child on a dark and stormy night, or as the result of some wicked thought you may have had. The child you bore came to you whole. God knew your child before you did, and, as with all His creations, God knew His child was good.

Although I speak of male homosexuals, I am well aware of female homosexuals. However, from my point of view, they are not harassed with the same fervor because women do not pose a threat to the patriarchy. For one thing, women lack the requisite and threatening power tool. Basically, man has dismissed homosexual women just as he, not God, has dismissed women since the days of Genesis, when God created Eve as Adam's equal in holding dominion over all the Earth.

Of course, I also know that men are parents of homosexual children. Yet, a homosexual male is somehow an egregious insult to a father, who may bellow something like "Not in my house!" For this reason, I don't know what to say to a man, because, once man declares his position on any topic, he is unlikely to relent. Besides that, men usually do not listen to women.

So, I am speaking to Mom. Dad can listen in. God entrusted women with the rearing of His children, of carrying life from one generation to another, of establishing the wholeness of His children. I have 60+ years of experience, as a mom. Woman may have come from man's body, but all of mankind comes from woman. God entrusted Ruth and Naomi to raise the lineage that would give us King David and Jesus Christ. You, Mother, are the Leah, the Rachael, and the Ruth to the line of humankind He has entrusted to you to nourish in heart and soul.

He gave you a homosexual child. So, what? That child is no different from any other child in your keeping. God brought him to you as, for example, a right- handed, left-brained, and brown-eyed boy. Your other child is heterosexual, left- handed, right-brained, and blue-eyed girl. So, what? In God's eyes, He loves each in the same way. A child of His is just that, a child of His. He knows each child before it becomes a seed in a mother's womb, your womb.

Let that "So, what?" remind you that in the Book of Matthew Jesus performed a "So, what?" moment with the centurion who came to him to heal his servant. Although Jesus understood that the servant probably was a sexual intimate of the centurion, he did not, in any way, rebuke him for having an intimate male partner. Rather, Jesus praised the centurion before the crowd for his profound faith in Him. Our unconditional faith is all He asks of any of us.

Do you sincerely believe that God created and sent you a

sample of the proverbial "junk" to your womb? Did He really make a mistake with your child? Of course not!

From what source are you receiving the information that has your brain tied in knots, suffering wrongly because someone declared your homosexual child a sin against God? Do you really believe in your heart that God would create a pile of sin in your womb for you to suffer over? When did you adopt silliness as your guide?

My guess is that you have heard this condemnation from a "friend." One you have trusted for years and probably was raised in a "strong Christian home." Another loaded-but-worthless, catch phrase. She listened to her daddy as a child, and now she hears the voice of her new master—her husband, and, of course, another voice of authority, her pastor. Tellingly, she has questioned nothing of what they have told her. My dear sister in Christ, do not suffer embarrassment or shame for your child because of your friend's ungodly malevolence. Celebrate his God-given uniqueness with joyful purpose.

In this case, your friend is not a friend. She/he is a gossip monger, carrying tales from some willfully ignorant man of God. It's time to tell her, "Get thee behind me, Satan!" Send her off to harass some other victim. If she is carrying tales about man's presumption that God created a mistake, then ask yourself, "Is this what Jesus would say to me? Is my friend really a Christian? Does she glorify God with her condemnation of my child?" To be sure, not all of Satan's messengers are women. Man easily wins that challenge.

Nevertheless, based upon my years of observations, women generally fall into line behind some male "minister" and believe every word he spews from his pulpit, wherever that pulpit may be. I assert this observation because when I ask "church women," why they think as they do, they generally answer with, "That's what Pastor Soandso said, and I believe him."

"Do you ever question him about anything?"

"No. I trust him. He's been my pastor for years."

Because man has denied woman the equality that God granted her in The Creation and has persuaded her, erroneously, that she is to remain silent, she dutifully repeats his point of view. The premise must be true if "he" said it.

I have no way of knowing where you are on this slippery slope of knowledge, but do you run your life according to God's Word, or according to public opinion? As His trusted child, He anointed you to be the mother of His new child. He blessed you with a heart of love abundant because a mother faces many challenges as she guides her child to his majority. Over time you learn that God's love is the foundation of your strength.

Your child came to you with everything he needs to grow and to flourish in your love and in God's. It is your job to nourish him, to love him, and to foster the parts that make him uniquely him. And, with the grace of God, you will help him to grow to his fullness.

If God had wanted you or anyone else to change or to cure your child from his affliction, He would have included instructions with the umbilical cord. I think you found none.

And, please, don't even consider packing your child off to some camp to be subjected to the aversion or the conversion therapy because some "minister" recommends it. The American Psychiatric Association and the American Psychological Association have declared, firmly, that these therapies do not work, and they are dangerous to your child's wellbeing. (An explanation of these therapies follows this chapter under a separate title.) There is nothing for you to change. Embrace him, encourage him to grow into his abilities. Celebrate for him and with him.

You know what, Mom and Dad? It is no one's business what your child's sexual persuasion is. Whatever prompted the destructive campaign, the ugly crusade against homosexuals, is a man-made perversion. The Bible, whatever version you hold dear, did not originally support man's pursuit of homosexuals.

Man discovered the word homosexual, and it became his oil, gushing for him to exploit. I could find no real explanation for the crusade, but, as I wrote in Chapter 3, I suspect it had something to do with the Devil's Joystick. Based upon my research, everything from the beginning of time and man's place in it has revolved around the DJ. With great pleasure and purpose, Satan has used man's obsession with that part of his anatomy to inflict the needless pain and shame and unwarranted deaths of homosexuals. And, by extension, the unwarranted abuse of women. Satan's seductive touch incites the unnecessary cruelty and anguish against the parents of homosexuals. Satan must be well pleased with his seductions.

Perhaps man, quite simply, fears that some homosexual will sneak up on him and cause harm to his manhood. Worse yet, the homosexual could force him into a sexual encounter which might result in penetration and his fall from manly grace.

My final thoughts to you, my reader, are these: Trust God. With your trust and faithfulness, He promised good for you, for all of us. Talking about your child in any way other than as another of your beloved normal children inflates his difference. Your child's difference is a normal genetic difference, not an ugly wart to be excised from the end of his nose. The God Wannabes, as they revel in their pious ignorance, have demonized a word they do not understand. They have assigned grievous, harmful meaning to a simple word and fostered homophobia.

I urge you, too, to read some of the resources I have provided. I am confident in my research and in my reporting, but I know from my history with women and women's groups, that women respond more readily to the male voice for "truth." I clearly am not male and have no interest in being male.

Nevertheless, I know from experience, that when you speak your own words from a base of knowledge, you will embrace a reassuring level of satisfaction and courage. You won't be thinking about how to respond to the busybody. More than that, when you have your own words for your child's place in God's world, that your child is everything God created him to be, you will stand taller and be more confident. Your love will glow from your heart and your new confidence.

When the next God Wannabes imposes their foolish, bogus accusations about how God made a mistake with your precious child, laugh and send them on their way. Don't waste your energy trying to dissuade them from their claims. They are embarrassments to God's world of goodness and light. Perhaps they are the authentic Sodomites.

On the other hand, God, who gifted you with another unique child of His, holds you firmly in His love.

Some closing thoughts:

Here we are. Working part of God's plan. Yes, that is what we are doing. I was called to the task of writing this book, you with reading it. No, this is not a coincidence. God does not trade in coincidences. We are part of the evolution of His grand plan. Each of us is where He wants us to be, doing what He wants us to do.

I have purposely repeated information about the word homosexual, when it was born, and its inclusion in the Bible. I wanted to make sure the that the God Wannabes could not just sweep my words under their mental rugs in their need to be right. Other repetitions are purposeful, too. Important messages often take more than one notice to become a significant, a lasting thought. This practice comes from my days as a journalist.

Repeating and summarizing the important details of any news story helped us to ensure that each reader had the full story. We could not be sure that today's reader had read the first day of reporting on a continuing news story. So, just as we repeated the salient facts of every news story, I have repeated the salient facts of this story in several chapters.

The God Wannabes kind of remind me of the time when I was about six or seven. Not quite old enough to know better but real close to that age. In my childish willfulness, I had provoked

Mother to the edge of her patience. I can't recall what I had done to stir her up so much, but I do remember that I had defied my mother. My defiance was about to get my hide tanned with a full measure of my mother's wrath. I was not going to wait around to be turned over her lap.

I bolted from the house and started running across the newly plowed field, toward my happy place in the apple orchard. I was running hard and kicking up bits of dirt with my bare feet. As I ran, my mother's voice trailed behind me. "I will be right here when you come home." I knew that. I was only delaying the inevitable. She and the hide-tanning would be waiting.

This is one thing you and I both know for certain. Our Father will be right there when the gossipmongers, the deadly abusers of God's homosexual children come home on judgment day. I suspect, though, that He might be more forgiving than my Mother. Hide-tanning isn't His style.

I am giving Prof. Gerald West and Peter in Acts 10: 34-35 (New International Version, NIV) the last words on the topic of homosexuality.

Prof. West, Senior Professor of Biblical Studies at the University KwaZulu-Natal, was present when Pope Francis delivered his statement supporting the rights of homosexuals and the truth that condemning homosexuals is wrong.

After the Pope's visit to /South Sudan in Africa, Prof. West summarized the Pope's statement which, by coincidence, captures the basic assertion of my nonfiction story. "As a biblical scholar, I would suggest that church leaders who use their cultures and theology to exclude homosexuals don't read Scripture carefully. Instead, they allow their patriarchal fears to distort it, seeking to find in the Bible proof-texts that will support attitudes of exclusion."[59]

Then "Peter began to speak: 'I now realize how true it is that God does not show favoritism but accepts from every nation the one who fears him and does what is right.'"

Amen to both statements.

∽

If the words and the thoughts in this nonfiction story anger you, insult you, make you uncomfortable, talk to God. He has been waiting to have this conversation.

God called me to be His scribe. I didn't write these words for myself, so your anger and your verbal abuse belong to God. You have betrayed man's trust and God's. Your argument is with God.

If you are satisfied with my words, even happy and relieved because of them, then, I, too, am happy. Praise God for your release from guilt, for your freedom from man's corrupt thinking.

One other specter must be dealt with. Because I have been so direct about man's part in the deception of God's word, the chant that I am a "man hater" will soon dominate. Man does not like to be called out. However, man has, from the beginning of time, overseen everything biblical. So, it is impossible to hold anyone else to account for their biblical dishonesty.

Hate is a waste of energy. My attention has centered on man because he has used his place of power to manipulate Scripture.

Hate also is a useless emotion. How can anyone hate someone who serves Satan, in the name of God?

Instead, I pray for the God Wannabe. I pray that he will focus his energy on serving and loving his neighbor, not taking his spirit from him. I pray that God will bless him the knowledge and understanding that he is dancing to Satan's seductive allure. I pray, too, that man realizes, as Peter said, God does not engage in favoritism, and man's words cannot change that truth.

As He declared in the beginning, His creations are good, very good.

The Truth about Aversion and Conversion Therapies

For decades, homosexuals, usually children of parents who want their children to be "normal," have been subjected to one of two therapies to "cure" them. The professionals say that the therapies don't cure anything, but they may well result in long-lasting mental and emotional side effects. Even suicide resulting from depression and anxiety.

I am providing the basic descriptions of the two therapies for your awareness. I am not qualified to comment. During my research for *It's Okay to be Gay*, I learned that, even though the American Psychiatric Association and the American Psychological Association have deemed the therapies ineffective and dangerous, they continue to be recommended. Forewarned is forearmed. The therapies can be barbaric.

I am using the words from some internet sites and providing those sites so that you can begin your search for more complete information. The available sites are numerous.

Conversion therapy "is any emotional or physical therapy used to 'cure' or 'repair' a person's attraction to the same sex, or their gender identity and expression." Providers of this therapy say they can make someone heterosexual or "straight." Scientists say there's no evidence to support this claim. Medical and mental health experts have rejected conversions therapy practices as dangerous and discriminatory for decades. It not only doesn't work, but it could lead to depression, anxiety, drug use, homelessness, and suicide. In extreme cases, the practices may be violent or torturous.

https://www.webmd.com/sex-relationships/
what-is-conversion-therapy

An offshoot of these techniques was "aversion therapy," which was founded on the premise that if LGBTQ people became disgusted by homosexuality, they would no longer experience same-sex desire. Under medical supervision, people were given chemicals that made them vomit when they, for example, looked at photos of their lovers. Others were given electrical shocks—sometimes to their genitals—while they looked at gay pornography or cross-dressed. (Note: Although the practices continue, it is unclear if genital shocks continue to be used.)

https://www.history.com/news/
gay-conversion-therapy-origins-19th-century

Aversion therapy uses conditioning but focuses on creating a negative response to an undesirable stimulus, such as drinking alcohol or using drugs. (Note: This therapy is used primarily for curing chemical addictions but has been adapted to treat homosexuality.)

Methods that have been used for aversion therapy include electric shock, other physical shocks (like from a rubber band snapping), an unpleasant smell or taste, negative imagery, and shame. (Note: the places at which the therapies are carried out frequently have the appearance that they are religion sponsored.)

https://simplypsychology.org/aversion-therapy.html

NAMI (National Alliance on Mental Illnesses) believes that no one should be subject to practices that can cause or worsen mental health symptoms. NAMI supports public policies and laws to ban the discredited, discriminatory, and harmful practice of conversion therapy.

https://www.nami.org/Advocacy/Policy-Priorities/
Stopping-Harmful-Practices/Conversion-Therapy

**Your discovery is limited only
by your desire to know.**

Resources

1. Minter, Kelly. RUTH *loss, love & legacy*. Nashville. LifeWay Press. 2009.

2. West, Gerald. *What does the Bible say about homosexuality? For starters, Jesus wasn't a homophone*. THE CONVERSATION. 2023. February. 9. 2023. March. https://theconversation.com/what-does-the-bible-say-about-homosexuality-for-starters-jesus-wasnt-a-homophobe-199424

3. *Fast Facts about American Religion*. The Hartford Institute for Religion Research. 2000-2021. 2022. March. http://hirr.hartsem.edu/research/fastfacts/fast_facts.html#numcong

4. Pavlovitz, John. Remember, *The Bible Never Mentions Building a Church*. Sermons by LOGOS. 2019. June. 24. http://JohnPavlovitz.com

5. Ortlund, Raymond C., Jr. *Male-Female Equality and Male Headship*. Recovering Biblical Manhood and Womanhood. 2009, February, 2. 2022. May. https://bible.org/seriespage/3-male-female-equality-and-male-headship-genesis-1-3

6. Spencer, Aida Bensanon. *Beyond the Curse Women Called to Ministry*. Hendrickson Publishers. 1985. pp 21.

7. Kunkle, Brett. *Challenge Response: The Bible Says Men are Superior to Men*. Stand to Reason Clear Thinking Christianity. 2016, February 2. 2022, October. 2016, February 2. 2022, October. https://www.str.org/w/challenge-response-the-bible-says-men-are-superior-to-women

8. Ibid.

9. Payne, Philip B., *"The Bible Teaches the Equal Standing of Man and Woman."* Priscilla Papers. Vol. 29), No.1 (Winter 2015)

10. *The purpose and meaning of the Third Commandment.* The Ten
    Commandments. 2021, February.
    https://www.the-tencommandments.org/third_commandment.html#:~:
    text=The%20New%20Revised%20Standard%20Version%20trans-
    lates%20the%20Third,will%20not%20acquit%20anyone%20who%20
    misuses%20his%20name

11. Tang, GVGK. *150 years ago, the word "homosexual" was coined in a
    secret correspondence.* 2018. May 6, 2021. April.
    https://medium.com/@gvgktang/150-years-ago-the-word-homosexual-
    was-coined-in-a-secret-correspondence-1803ff9a79bc

12. *Constructing the Heterosexual, Homosexual, Bisexual System, by New
    Katz.* OutHistory It's about time. 2021, April. 2023, May 26, 2023.
    https://outhistory.org/exhibits/show/heterohomobi/merriam

13. Rogers, Jack. *Jesus, the Bible and Homosexuality. Exp13.lode the
    Myths, Heal the Church* Louisville. Westminster John Knox Press.
    2009. Pp 129.

14. Ibid 130.

15. Greenough, Chris. *Using the Bible Against* LGBTQ+ *people is an Abuse
    ofScripture.* The Conversation. 2020, January 28. 2022, December.

16. Parks-Weekly, Romell. https://www.facebook.com/pastorparksweekly/

17. Helminiak, Daniel A. *What the Bible Really Says About Homosexuality.*
    Milleniali Edition. New Mexico. Alamo Square Press. 2000. pp 54

18. Wilson, Nancy. *Outing the Bible Queer Folks, God, Jesus, and the
    Christian Scriptures.* LifeJourney Press. 1994. pp 54.

19. Helminiak, Daniel A. *What the Bible Really Says About Homosexuality.*
    Milleniali Edition. New Mexico. Alamo Square Press. 2000. pp 54.

20. Rogers, Jack. *Jesus, the Bible and Homosexuality. Explode the
    Myths, Heal the Church.* Louisville. Westminster John Knox Press.
    2009. pp 69.

21. Oxford, Ed. *Has 'Homosexual' Always Been in the
    Bible?* United MethodistInsight. 2019, October. 2021,
    November.   https://um-insight.net/perspectives/
    has-%E2%80%9Chomosexual%E2%80%9D-always-been-in-the-bible/

22. Ibid.

23. Ibid.

24. Helminiak, Daniel. A. *What the Bible Really Says About Homosexuality.* New Mexico. Alamo Square Press. 2000. pp 18.

25. Ibid.

26. Rogers, Jack. *Jesus, the Bible and Homosexuality. Explode the Myths, Heal the Church.* Louisville. Westminster John Knox Press. 2009. pp 130.

27. Rogers, Jack. *Jesus, the Bible and Homosexuality. Explode the Myths, Heal the Church.* Louisville. Westminster John Knox Press. 2009. pp 61.

28. Oxford, Ed. *Has "Homosexual" Always been in the Bible?* Forge. 2019, March 3. 2022, June 6. https://www.forgeonline.org/blog/2019/3/8/what-about-romans-124-27

29. Ibid.

30. Wills, Matthew. *The Codpiece and the Pox.* JSTOR Daily. 2019, May 30. 2022. https://daily.jstor.org/the-codpiece-and-the-pox/

31. Davis, Julia. *Six Penis Panics Around the World.* Mental Floss. 2016, January 28. https://www.mentalfloss.com/article/72227/6-penis-panics-around-world

32. Ibid.

34. Rampton, Mike. Why are There So Many Ancient Fountains Featuring Little Boys Peeing? Mental Floss.. 2022, June 8. 2022, November. https://www.mentalfloss.com/posts/why-ancient-fountains-feature-boys-peeing

35. Oxford, Ed. *Has "Homosexual" Always been in the Bible?* Forge. 2019, March 3. 2022, June 6. https://www.forgeonline.org/blog/2019/3/8/what-about-romans-124-27

36. Akpan, Nsikan. There is no 'gay gene.' There is no 'straight gene.' Sexuality is just complex, study confirms. Science magazine. 2019, August 29. 2021, July.

37. Rogers, Jack. *Jesus, the Bible and Homosexuality. Explode the Myths, Heal the Church.* Louisville. Westminster John Knox Press. 2009. pp 59.

38. Milar, Katharine S. The myth buster. Time Capsule. 2011, February. 2021, March. https://www.google.com/ search?client=fire fox-b-1-d&q=The+myth+buster+Evelyn+Hooker

39. Bagemihl, Bruce. *Biological Exuberance: Animal Homosexuality and Natural Diversity.* New York. St. Martin's Press. 1999.

40. Percula clownfish. National Aquarium. 2022, May. https://aqua.org/explore/animals/percula-clownfish

41. Yam, Philip. *Strange but True: Komodo Dragons Show that "Virgin Births"* are Possible. Scientific American. 2006, December 28. 2022, February. https://www.scientificamerican.com/article/ strange-but-true-komodo-d/

42. Elbein, Asher. *Newly Recorded Condor 'Virgin Birth' is Another Way Birds are Like Reptiles.* National Audubon Society. 2021, November 10. 2022, February. https://www.audubon.org/news/ newly-recorded-condor-virgin-birth- another-way-birds-are-reptiles

43. How do slugs mate? BBC Wildlife magazine. 2022, November 8. 2022, February. https://www.discoverwildlife.com/animal-facts/ insects- invertebrates/how-do-slugs-mate/

44. The Mysterious Living Stones of Romania: They Grow and Move. Geologyin. 2023. 2023, January. https://www.geologyin.com/2018/04/ the-mysterious-living-stones-of-romania.html

45. Minter, Kelly. RUTH *loss, love and legacy.* Nashville. LifeWay Press. 2009.'

46. Ibid.

47. Ibid.

48. DeMoss, Nancy Leigh. *Ruth The Message of Redemption & Revival in the Book of Ruth.* A Video Bible Study for Small Groups. Workbook. Buchanan. Published by Revive Our Hearts. 2002.

49. Schierer, Priscilla. *And We are* CHANGED *Encounters with a Transforming God.* Chicago. Moody Publishers. 2003. pp 166.

50. Ibid. pp 145.

51. Ibid.

52. Minter, Kelly. RUTH *loss, love & legacy.* Nashville. LifeWay Press. 2009.

53. Miner, Jeff. *Ruth loved Naomi as Adam loved Eve.* Would Jesus Descriminate? 2020, December 24. 2021, February. http://www.wouldjesusdiscriminate.org/biblical_evidence/ruth_naomi.html

54. Ibid.

55. Helminiak, Daniel A.*What the Bible Really Says About Homosexuality.* New Mexico. Alamo Square Press. 2000. pp 128.

56. Ibid.

57. Ibid

58. Miner, Jeff. *Ruth loved Naomi as Adam loved Eve.* Would Jesus Descriminate? 2020, December 24. 2021, February. http://www.wouldjesusdiscriminate.org/biblical_evidence/ruth_naomi.html

59. West, Gerald. What does the Bible say about homosexuality? For starters, Jesus wasn't a homophone. THE CONVERSATION. 2023. February. 9. 2023. March. http://Theconversation.com/what-does-the- bible-say-about-homosexuality-for- starters-jesus-wasn't-a-homophobe-199424